T0300205

Demystifying Communications Risk

*Dedicated to Petra, Cleo, Luca, Ana and Kim with thanks
for their patience, love and support.*

Demystifying Communications Risk

A Guide to Revenue Risk
Management in the
Communications Sector

MARK JOHNSON

Routledge
Taylor & Francis Group

LONDON AND NEW YORK

First published 2012 by Gower Publishing

Published 2016 by Routledge
2 Park Square, Milton Park, Abingdon, Oxfordshire OX14 4RN
711 Third Avenue, New York, NY 10017, USA

First issued in paperback 2016

Routledge is an imprint of the Taylor & Francis Group, an informa business

Copyright © 2012 Mark Johnson

Mark Johnson has asserted his moral right under the Copyright, Designs and Patents Act, 1988, to be identified as the author of this work.

All rights reserved. No part of this book may be reprinted or reproduced or utilised in any form or by any electronic, mechanical, or other means, now known or hereafter invented, including photocopying and recording, or in any information storage or retrieval system, without permission in writing from the publishers.

Notice:
Product or corporate names may be trademarks or registered trademarks, and are used only for identification and explanation without intent to infringe.

British Library Cataloguing in Publication Data
Johnson, Mark.
  Demystifying communications risk : a guide to revenue risk
  management in the communications sector.
  1. Telecommunication--Management. 2. Risk management.
  3. Fraud--Prevention.
  I. Title
  384'.068-dc23

Library of Congress Cataloging-in-Publication Data
Johnson, Mark.
  Demystifying communications risk : a guide to revenue risk management in
  the communications sector / by Mark Johnson.
     p. cm.
  Includes bibliographical references and index.
  ISBN 978-1-4094-2941-8 (hbk)
1. Digital communications. 2. Risk management. I. Title.
  TK5103.7.J64 2012
  384.068'1--dc23

                                                                    2012011041

ISBN 13: 978-1-138-27893-6 (pbk)
ISBN 13: 978-1-4094-2941-8 (hbk)

Contents

List of Figures

List of Tables

About the Author

Mark Johnson first became involved in high technology risk management in the late 1980s when he joined Cable & Wireless as a communications fraud manager. Prior to this he had served as a military officer engaged primarily in narcotics enforcement operations in the Caribbean.

At Cable & Wireless, Mark designed and managed the development of one of the industry's first automated fraud management software systems. This experience led to him being recruited or hired as a consultant by a number of major firms, including Alcatel, Nortel and Ericsson. In 2001 Mark setup his own consulting business, The Risk Management Group, and he and his associates have been providing consultancy, product design and training services via that channel ever since.

Mark lives in Cambridgeshire with his family. *Demystifying Communications Risk* is his first book, but he has already started work on a second that attempts to demystify the subjects of cyber security and digital intelligence.

FOREWORD

By Lord Toby Harris

Demystifying Communications Risk

Towards the end of 2004, I started asking questions in the House of Lords about how secure the UK's critical national infrastructure was against cyber attack and even initiated a short debate on the subject. The Ministerial responses were always reassuring, if bland. The assessment – I was told – was that the risks were not high and that in any case there were robust arrangements in place to deal with any eventualities.

I was not convinced, tabled more questions, and began asking regularly how many computers had been compromised in each government department in the previous year. The answers were fairly meaningless but it was disconcerting to hear – implausibly – that most departments had not been aware of any problems at all.

I knew that things had changed and that the issue was now at least being taken seriously, when after a couple of years, the responses changed to a blanket refusal to answer on the basis that supplying such information might be helpful to the country's enemies.

In 2010 cyber attacks on infrastructure appeared in the National Risk Register accompanying the National Security Strategy and now, of course, 'hostile attacks upon UK cyber space by other states and large scale cyber crime' appear as one of the four Tier One risks in the latest version of that Strategy.

However, I suspect that for many businesses – even now – awareness of cyber risk is rather like that of the UK government in 2004: they do not see it as a major threat and anyway they believe they are adequately protected. Too often, cyber security is seen as just an IT matter and not something that those in charge of the business itself should take seriously.

Sadly, they will only do so in some of those cases after the business has suffered some significant or even catastrophic loss as a result of an information security failure.

Cyber security risks are only one facet of a wider set of issues affecting the communications sector. Apart from technical attacks, there are also numerous types of fraud against businesses and consumers, together with identity theft and other data protection challenges. In addition, revenue can be lost due to technical faults and business process failures. These all add up to a wide, varied and complex mix of threats that the modern business needs to manage. And as the recent phone hacking scandal revealed, it is not only business and government that stands to suffer from security failures, but the citizen as well.

The threat comes from many sources. At one end of the spectrum are the cyber juvenile delinquents operating from a bedroom in their parents' home trying to demonstrate their own technical skill to their peers. They may merely want to penetrate a system to leave a calling card and to demonstrate, like Kilroy, that they have been there. Any damage may be accidental, but may also have an impact on a business's reputation with its customers and suppliers.

However, at the other end, there will be those who are trying to do serious damage, such as some cyber criminals, or to benefit significantly financially as in the case of telecoms fraudsters. Raising awareness of how poorly defined controls contribute to the threat is a key first step in developing solutions.

The last year or so has also seen the growth of 'hactivism' with those wanting to make a political point using cyber means, including extensive use of social media, and many businesses – fairly or unfairly – have suffered embarrassment or worse as a result.

Then there is the organised theft of intellectual property or sensitive information. This is often covert and there may be no obvious sign that it has happened – until a competitor starts to use the information obtained to the detriment of its original owner. There is no doubt that this is happening on a huge scale with many household-name companies and organisations having been victims.

And then there are the organised criminals, seeking to extract or extort money from those who have not adequately protected themselves, to move funds through unregulated channels, or to obtain anonymous communications capabilities through telecom fraud, so as to avoid lawful surveillance.

Vulnerabilities are not all technical: however secure a system is and however good the protection software is, the system still has to be used by individuals. And those individuals may become disaffected or may be suborned or may simply be careless. Even the best employee's keenness to work at home or on the move may inadvertently introduce a weakness.

These threats are all part of the new normality, the environment in which businesses have to operate in the second decade of the twenty-first century. The lesson is simple. We all have to adjust to this new normality. And that means that we must all take information security far more seriously.

> Lord Toby Harris is a member of the House of Lords and of the Joint Committee on National Security. He is Chair of the All-Party Parliamentary Group on Policing. Professionally, he runs his own public affairs consultancy which advises a number of major corporations and organisations.

Preface

Any sufficiently advanced technology is indistinguishable from magic.

Arthur C. Clarke

THE CASE OF THE FRAUDULENT TRAFFIC LIGHTS

A few years ago, we watched as a major mobile phone operator installed a clever new system for automating the management of the traffic lights in one major city. This was a high profile trial and the operator in question was fitting mobile telecommunications gear to each light, so that remote management and control of the lights was possible via the telephone network.

Unfortunately, and against the best advice, the operator opted not to restrict the SIM cards in these lights to specific data services and number ranges. The result was that the SIMs provided the full range of voice and data services normally associated with a 3G account. No sooner had the engineers left the scene but several hundred traffic lights were broken into and the SIM cards taken. Substantial volumes of fraudulent calls were then made to destinations as far flung as Asia, the UK and the USA, reportedly costing the operator several hundred thousand dollars in the course of a day.

The example above was yet another demonstration of something that I have been observing for years – no matter how clever you think you're being, somebody out there has already figured out a way to rip you off. While the integrity of others is desired, it is never assumed, and a small minority can tear the financial heart out of a business in an instant, if you give them the opportunity to do so.

While this is true in most sectors, it is particularly true in the communications sector. Characterised as it is by huge numbers of subscribers and complex services based on technologies manufactured and delivered by third party suppliers, as well as a vast interwoven global network of voice and data links and platforms, the modern communications market has never been more exposed to risk. These risks go beyond fraud and security to include malware, identity theft, data disclosure, revenue leakage due to errors and omissions, and even industrial espionage.

I came to the communications risk management sector by accident and by way of the War on Drugs, a failed US-led attempt to curtail the inexorable spread of illegal narcotics from suppliers in Latin America and Asia to consumers in Europe and North America. My time as a soldier and later a security contractor in this low intensity but bloody conflict was spent in the Caribbean, chiefly Jamaica and the Port of Miami, with short assignments that took me to the sea ports of several other drug exporting nations.

My military service was as an infantry officer in one of the regional defence forces, eventually commanding a rifle company of 120 men on drug enforcement operations in support of the US Drug Enforcement Administration (DEA). Our role was to provide the armed muscle for interdiction in response to intelligence gathered by DEA agents about planned or ongoing drug trafficking operations.

A typical raid involved us loading our troops into helicopters to be dropped off in the dark on one of a hundred illegal airstrips hacked out of the bush and scrub. Sometimes we would find nothing but tire treads and footprints. At other times there would be an aircraft, several pickup trucks and men armed with automatic rifles on the landing strip. The pickups would be packed with bales of locally produced marijuana or, less frequently, packages of cocaine being transhipped from Colombia to Florida. We would seize these, and hand them over to the national Police for processing, along with our prisoners. Cases would either go to court or not, depending on whom the police officers were affiliated to and which local politician decided to get involved. In the main, the wheels of justice turned, if slowly, and most offenders would spend the next several years in a hot, crowded and violent Caribbean prison.

A move to more routine cargo examination operations in a major containerised cargo port provided the anti-climax to six years of infantry operations. This was less hazardous to life and limb and intellectually more challenging as we attempted to detect the myriad ways in which the cleverer drug exporters would conceal their contraband in commercial cargo or on large ocean going vessels. We learned that there were hundreds of ways to do this successfully and our searches made use of trained teams, dogs and even divers to inspect the hulls of each vessel.

We were required to profile shippers, shipments, vessels and their crews, looking for links in the document trail that might trigger suspicion about a particular cargo container out of the 10,000 or more moving through the port in any given period. And we found more than narcotics. Smuggled cars, firearms and ammunition, people and almost anything else of value on the open market would be uncovered with alarming regularity. I began to appreciate how deeply interwoven with the fabric of daily life criminal activity can be, and how central transactional data analytics was becoming to effective crime intelligence operations.

The age of mobile communications and the internet had arrived and with it came new forms of crime. Meanwhile, my work on containerised cargo procedures and tracking had attracted some attention from a leading 'big 4' accounting and consultancy firm. One of their clients was the main telecoms company in the country and this firm was experiencing huge rises in levels of communications fraud by both outsiders and by staff, as well as revenue leakage from their increasingly complex systems. I was offered a position as a consultant in this completely new field. Being a one eyed man in the kingdom of the blind has always had great appeal to me and I leapt at the opportunity, not letting my total ignorance of telecom or computer technologies slow me down for a moment. I needn't have worried.

While the road from drug enforcement to revenue assurance, fraud control and cyber security may appear to be a route from the exotic to the mundane, nothing could be further from the truth and within weeks of starting my new assignment, I had grasped some important fundamentals:

1.   Crime is crime; the motivations of perpetrators and their behavioural characteristics are very similar across different classes of criminal enterprise.

2.   Dissimilar crime types are often linked; the drug trafficker needs anonymous telephone services, obtained illicitly. The money launderer had to get his funds somewhere, often from drug sales or fraud. This meant that my past experience was of value in the new role.

3.   There are patterns that highlight suspect activity in most kinds of transactional data, be it flight patterns for drug-laden aircraft, the movement of cargo containers, suspicious financial transactions

or fraudulent telephone calls. The rudimentary lessons I had learned about data analytics would prove to be very valuable in the communications sphere.

4.   While narcotics crimes have a deleterious effect on the fabric of society, a successful attack on our information and communications technology (ICT) infrastructure, or a series of fatal errors or technical failures, would tear that fabric to shreds.

Eventually, I came to realise something else; errors and omissions are as common, if not more common as crime as a cause of financial loss for major communications firms. The gap between the skills and expertise of most staff and the complexity of the systems and processes they are responsible for is increasing across the board. In many firms, the great majority of employees regard the core technologies that support the business as 'black boxes', the inner workings of which are indistinguishable from magic, to paraphrase Arthur C. Clarke.

I also recognised that the increasing reliance of communications firms on IP and cyber technologies would mean that cyber security would become an equally important facet of risk management and that the traditional model wherein credit, fraud, leakage and cyber/IT security are handled by separate parts of the business was unsustainable over the long term and their consolidation within, or synchronisation by, a single communications risk organisation was the only logical outcome. In an era in which we are utterly dependent on ICT for almost all commercial, financial and governmental processes, not to mention our social networks and entertainment channels, threat actors and risks that affect those technologies assume strategic proportions.

This book is intended to explain how these risks have manifested themselves in the recent past and how they are evolving. It deals with fraud, leakage and some aspects of cyber security as they relate to convergent communications networks and attempts to provide examples that will aid the layman and the practitioner alike. My goal has not been to expose commercial secrets or to embarrass the many who work diligently to mitigate these risks every day, rather it is to highlight the hidden battle these professionals fight and to underscore its importance for all of us.

This, therefore, is a book about communications risk, but it is not a guide to would-be fraudsters. The purpose of the book is to raise awareness of the multi-faceted and often complex forms that operational revenue risks take in the communications sector. Whether the issue is fraud, inaccurate billing, bypass and arbitrage, credit fraud, malware or unregulated e-Payments, awareness of staffers, customers, shareholders and regulators is the key to prevention or control.

And yet, there is no profit without a degree of risk taking. Avoidance, mitigation, management and even acceptance of risk have therefore been amongst the required responses for anyone playing in this sector. Operators have had to protect their revenue streams by developing some of the most sophisticated process controls and technical countermeasures in use anywhere in the private sector; pattern analysis, platform reconciliations, profiling, social media analytics, deep packet inspection, penetration testing and many other techniques are now used in combination to produce a bewildering array of alerts, case files and root cause analysis investigation reports.

A Word About Diagrams

Preventative measures and assurance audits add even more depth to the layers of security in place on most networks, meaning that the topic of communications risk has become almost impenetrable for anyone who is not deeply involved in its delivery and management. Nevertheless, all complexity arises from simplicity and a key ambition of this book to break down and explain the key aspects of modern communications risk for the benefit of both those working in the sector as well as the non-technical reader.

I have used a large number of simplistic illustrations to explain important concepts. Nevertheless, modern communications involves interactions between people and systems, and those people and systems operate in a complex, multi-faceted and three-dimensional real world context. No two-dimensional diagram can do more than express the essence of a thing, process or model. My approach to illustrations in this book has been to use the 'whiteboard' paradigm because the use of whiteboards to explain technical concepts and challenges is ubiquitous in the communications industry and it's something that really struck me when I first arrived. By drawing on a 'whiteboard', I hope to give the reader a true flavour of how cases are actually discussed within the business and how solutions are often devised or assessed.

A Word About Confidentiality

Particularly in the fraud section of the book, we were very aware of the need to maintain confidentiality in terms of the identities of the networks we have visited and also the specifics of some of the fraud cases we have witnessed. We have therefore concealed or altered the identity of all of the networks referenced and when it came to describing fraud cases, we developed the following rules:

- Provide a description that is sufficient to explain the general outlines of the risk scenario so as to make the case for specific controls, but without providing a 'How To' manual for would be fraudsters, hackers or other criminals.

- Describe risks that are common across the industry and for which descriptions are available in the public domain.

- Do not describe new risks in any detail, particularly in very new services that operators have not yet had a chance to get to grips with in security terms.

- Focus on explaining the essence of each risk class rather than describing all its practicalities in depth.

By so doing, we hope to provide a readable and engaging account of risk in communications services, without thereby exposing those services to increased risk through our efforts. My own hope is that the book will make some small contribution to security by raising awareness and, in particular, giving readers a framework for understanding the potential for risk in future technologies and services. I hope that we have succeeded in producing an informative and readable account of a 20-year risk management campaign that continues to this day and which can only become more complex and challenging as the years pass.

Mark Johnson
Cambridge

Acknowledgements

The opportunity to research and write this book was both a privilege and a learning experience. I am indebted to a long list of colleagues, past and present, for all of the ideas and knowledge set out here. There are simply too many to mention, or even to recall, as much of my 'research' stretches back over 35 years of professional life.

I would like to record my special thanks to Lord Toby Harris for his professional advice and guidance in general and also for agreeing to write the foreword to this work, to Dr Liliya Gelemerova for her contribution to the section on anti-money laundering controls and her kind editing of my own efforts in that area, to DCI Andrew Fyfe of the City of London Police, who taught me about the topics of bribery and corruption, to Nick Mann and Geoff Ibbett for their chapters on controlling employee fraud and revenue assurance risks, to Alan Blaney for his contributions in the area of telecom fraud and Jason Hart who supplied the text on penetration testing.

Finally, I would like to thank Petra, Cleo and Luca for their patient support and for leaving me to it as my mouse and keyboard clicked and clattered over the last 12 months.

1

Communications Fraud Control

Defining Telecom Fraud

Sometimes defined as 'a deception deliberately practiced to secure unfair or unlawful gain or to cause a loss', many jurisdictions define up to three types of dishonest act that may constitute fraud, as per the following examples:

- Making a false representation

- Failing to disclose information

- Abusing a position of trust

Generally speaking, the test that determines whether or not any of the above actions was fraudulent is the establishment of what may have been in the mind of the alleged fraudster, i.e. his intent. As this is subjective, the standard of what the reasonable man would have thought or felt in the same circumstances is applied. When applied to highly technical communications fraud cases, there is an additional challenge in that the fraud techniques applied may not be easily understood by the average person, as well as the advantage that detailed data about the case will often be available after the fact from the various technology platforms that support communications services.

In simple terms, people commit fraud *deliberately*. It is never accidental because it requires intent. So they do it by lying, faking or concealing in order to get something for themselves (or occasionally, as we shall see, for another) or to cause a loss to a person or organisation. Communications fraud is one of several types of financial crime, which include but are not limited to:

- 'White collar crime'

- Money laundering and terrorist financing

- Tax evasion

- Insider dealing and market abuse

- Fraud

- Cyber crime

- Corruption and bribery

Fraud itself can be further broken down into several types and, again, the list is not exhaustive:

- Corporate fraud

- Banking fraud

- Securities and investments fraud

- Insurance fraud

- Accounting fraud

- Credit fraud

- Payment fraud

- Online fraud

- Communications service fraud

- Intellectual property theft

Because people are complex and varied in their motives, skills, access to systems, determination, gullibility, personal networks and just about every other attribute, all we can predict is that there will be as many future fraud scenarios as there are future fraudsters and each case will be unique. While this makes detection and control challenging, we can nevertheless examine previous cases in order to determine the *nature* of fraud. Simply listing the common motives of fraudsters, derived from decades of case experience, illustrates the diversity of drivers:

- Criminal greed

- Financial need

- The intellectual challenge

- Revenge

- To conceal losses or errors

- Peer pressure or blackmail

- Opportunity and temptation

- And, in the case of telecom fraud, to create anonymous communications paths or to bypass state restrictions on communications

Our ability to combat fraud depends on our awareness of these motives as each fraud will be manifested in different ways depending on what drives the fraudster. Who the fraudster is will also affect how he (or she) commits the offence. As Figure 1.1 on the following page illustrates, fraudsters may come from one or more groups and any given case will often involve collusion between people from different parts of the business or from the outside:

- Owners, senior management or board members

- Middle management

- Other employees

- Contracted staff

- External parties, often in collusion with insiders:

- Consumers
- Organised fraud rings
- Suppliers
- Distributors or vendor channels

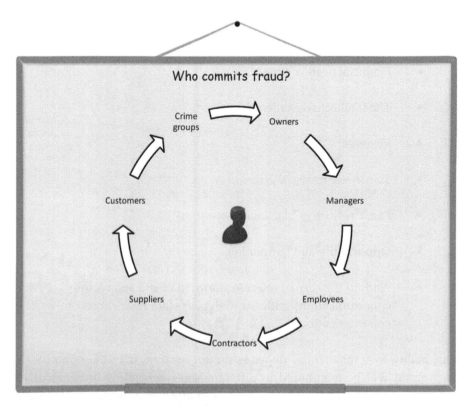

Figure 1.1   Who commits fraud?

In this chapter we will describe a number of examples of how fraud has manifested itself over the years, in fixed, data and mobile services. We have picked cases from a wide range of geographies and cultures. What you might experience in your region and circumstances may differ, but in most cases the principles of fraud and fraud management will be the same.

COMMUNICATIONS FRAUD VERSUS OTHER FINANCIAL FRAUDS

How does communications fraud differ from other financial frauds? The answer is that it differs less than one might first think. Traditional financial frauds involve the use of a financial product or service, such as cheques, credit cards, online banking, credit notes etc. to perpetrate a fraud that can be concealed from the average person. Some of these frauds are very complex and the most successful ones, or at least those with the greatest impact, have tended to involve financial products that only a small number of people understand. The less well understood the product, the easier it is to deceive for the purpose of gaining or to cause a loss.

Communications frauds also involve technically complex packages, products, applications or platforms, which are generally poorly understood by users and often by those supposedly managing them within the business. This is compounded by the fact that many communications services are built up through the combination of a number of separate elements, many of which will have been devised elsewhere and for other purposes. Any given employee may only be fully conversant with a few service components, depending on others to understand the remainder. So, a clever fraudster with superior technical knowledge can find gaps in coverage and exploit these in ways that the average employee is unlikely to detect, with intent to profit by this activity.

As we shall see, a requirement to demonstrate intent has significant implications for both systems and business processes, as evidence of human intentions generally lays beyond the traditional network-centric approach of telecom security professionals. This has caused the communications fraud management discipline to follow an evolutionary path that has made it increasingly customer and 'account' focused, a trend that can be expected to accelerate as complex next generation service offerings reach maturity. This trend takes fraud management into realms dominated by credit control and customer services teams, as well as marketing, while the ongoing need for network data and for technical countermeasures means that fraud teams have retained a firm base of operations within the network environment.

Fraud management, then, is a cross-functional discipline distinct from most others and functioning simultaneously as an operational team and as a practice more akin to internal audit than to a normal line function. This dual mode of working can create confusion and conflict, and many fraud teams have been forced to expend significant energy on communicating their roles and objectives to other departments within the same company. Moving fraud from the perceived position of 'company cop' to a place where it is recognised as a real contributor to corporate profits has taken many years of effort. One objective of this book is to reinforce that positioning by laying out the drivers for, and challenges faced by, fraud management operations in a straightforward fashion for the casual reader.

ACCESS VERSUS EXPLOITATION

A key point often overlooked is the distinction between fraudulent acts intended to provide access to services and the exploitation of that access. Each of these may take a number of forms and may be combined, one with the other, in different ways. When speaking of a fraud 'case' we should firstly always attempt to break it down into these components.

Generally speaking, *access frauds* (identity theft, subscription frauds, illegal activations by employees, etc.) are the focus of preventative business processes such as credit vetting or revenue assurance-type checks, audits and reconciliations. On the other hand, *exploitations* are addressed through technical efforts to detect suspect traffic patterns in as close to real time as possible. This relationship is illustrated in Figure 1.2 below. Two further considerations arise:

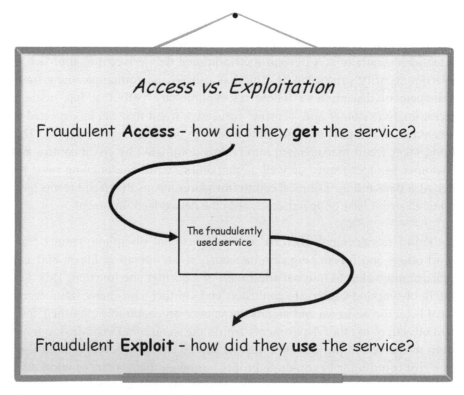

Figure 1.2   Access vs. exploitation

- Exploitations may be 'subscriber centric', meaning that they are carried out by a relatively small number of people whose calling patterns will stand out from the mass, or they may be 'wholesale' in nature (bypass frauds for example), meaning that an entire traffic stream involving thousands of individual subscribers or business accounts may consist of fraudulent traffic. Different detection techniques apply to each of these; Fraud Management System (FMS) based analysis for subscriber-centric frauds and call generation or traffic trending analysis approaches for wholesale frauds.

- 'Real time' analysis can result in an analysis window that is too small to support effective trend analysis. By definition, trends develop over time and it is therefore necessary to detect known types of suspect event (based on fraud intelligence) in close-to-real time, while retaining the ability to track other suspect trends over longer periods of time. There is no single approach to effective communications fraud management, or to use a phrase that was once widely spoken in the sector, 'There is no silver bullet'.

LINKS BETWEEN FRAUD AND OTHER REVENUE LOSSES

Fraud, as defined above, is not in and of itself an attack upon the operator's network. Rather, the commission of fraud is a goal which may be facilitated by a variety of apparently unrelated attacks. For example, in a scenario in which a hacker breaks into an operator's switches and then makes adaptations to settings which allow free calls to be made, the illegal access constitutes an attack that breaches access controls, the adaptations made are unauthorised (possibly illegal) alterations to settings, but no fraud occurs until the changes effected are *exploited* in order to make free calls or to obtain other services for which no payment will be made.

This complexity goes some way towards explaining the lingering practice within telecom operators in which network security, IT security, fraud management and other affected functional areas continue to work in isolation, often reporting to different senior managers. It is not uncommon to find security teams who are wholly professional and totally absorbed by the task of preventing hacking attacks, but who show little or no awareness of the frauds that may follow such intrusions, while conversely, the fraud manager may pursue individual fraud cases without a detailed understanding of, or even access to information about, the attacks that facilitated it. Not only does this make it less likely that the culprits will be caught, but it also increases the risk that connections between related incidents will be overlooked.

In converged, next generation networks offering 'Triple Play' (voice/video/ internet) or, more recently, 'Quad Play' (loosely defined as mobile voice/video/ internet plus fixed voice/video/internet on a single account), segmentation of tasks and focus in this manner will spell disaster for the overall security effort, The relationship between fraud control and other teams within the telecom operation must become better coordinated. Many operators have started to recognise this and it is increasingly common to hear of fraud and revenue assurance teams being consolidated. We also see network security and even credit control being brought into a single Risk Management Group structure.

One critical change in mindset that must occur is for all players within these disparate functions to recognise and explore both the relationship between motivation, attack and exploitation, and the necessary congruence of investigative processes and countermeasures. This is required in order to ensure that related case data are brought together in a way that supports end-to-end analysis of each scenario, and also to ensure that organisational responses to fraud and the facilitating attacks address both the causes and their effects.

NON-TECHNICAL REASONS FOR WHY FRAUD OCCURS

Socio-economic conditions are one of the primary drivers leading to some of the major classes of fraud. However, it is important to recognise that in many, if not most cases, those who are at the lower end of the socio-economic ladder are more likely to be exploited as a market segment by organised fraudsters than they are to commit the frauds themselves. Perhaps the most common scenario is 'call selling'. This involves an organised fraudsters setting up a bank of fixed or mobile telephones and offering cheap calls to a target group, for example an immigrant population concentrated in a small urban area. The fraudster has recognised that the combination of distance from home and lower wages creates an opportunity for him to sell illegal calls to this market segment.

Demographics and migration have therefore long been seen as important predictors of traditional voice fraud patterns and trends in the sense that where certain demographics profiles are evident the market opportunity for the organised fraudster is apparent. Monitoring and recognising these existing or emerging patterns can allow the fraud manager to work in a proactive way to minimise or at least detect predictable classes of fraud.

The penetration of technology has placed in the hands of an ever-growing number of subscribers new capabilities in terms of interaction with the network and subversion of business models and technological safeguards. As access to education grows apace with this access to new technologies the fraud threat along with other security threats becomes increasingly sophisticated. Today's fraud management teams are well aware of the complexity and sophistication of some of the emerging fraud challenges although it is also true that many of the older and more basic frauds continue to abound.

The challenge factor is another well known aspect of the fraud and security challenge. When we as an industry make claims about the impregnable nature of the security built into our products we essentially throw down the gauntlet to every hacker, 'phreaker' and fraudster out there in the wider world. A perfect example of just this scenario was the announcement made at the launch of GSM services to the effect that these were now so secure in terms of encryption that no one could penetrate the service. Although it has been claimed subsequently that these statements referred to encryption related to authentication, attacks were made within days of this publicity on the encryption governing the voice channel and this was duly breached. The fact that these attacks were made in response to the challenge laid down is made clear by the manner in which those responsible for breaching the security controls immediately moved to publicise their success. Indeed, in this instance the attackers were academics and students from a leading university. Nevertheless others who are less interested in publicity are equally motivated by the challenge factor.

Simple criminal greed is a primary factor driving most serious instances of fraud. The type of case that threatens an operator (i.e. large cases involving many thousands of transactions over many, many days) is almost always the result of an organised and sophisticated fraud attack launched by experienced persons often with access to the operators' systems or employees. It is organised attacks that constitute the greatest fraud threat to operators' revenues, but at the same time the fact that these attacks essentially represent the conduct of an unlawful business operation means that they have a certain profile – they are designed to generate a profit. The existence of a profile is a key factor for fraud control because the detection of suspicious activity hidden within huge volumes of transaction and call data is based on understanding and recognising profiles such as this. We can conclude from this that an awareness of the fraudster's business model and business case equips us with the basic intelligence we need to detect the resulting profile from within the transaction database.

A lack of corporate due diligence is a further important point as many fraud and security vulnerabilities are not only predictable and preventable but are actually known about before the frauds occur. Very often there is a failure at a management level to fully understand the business case for taking proactive steps to tackle fraud vulnerabilities. Senior managers are often ignorant of the real impact of fraud and it can be a struggle for those responsible operationally to get this message across to their superiors.

The Impact of Communications Fraud

There has been a long-running debate within the industry regarding the actual financial impact of fraud on an operator. Historically, fraud managers have pointed to the face value of bills written off as a measure of the cost of frauds associated with those accounts. However, as many financial controllers have stressed, most if not all of the calls appearing fraudulently on a bill would never have been made if the caller had expected to pay the cost of the calls. They conclude that there was never the potential to earn any substantial part of the revenue from these calls and therefore the face value of bills written off is not a true indication of the cost of the fraud to the operator.

These are valid arguments but they ignore a simple but important fact; even though the fraudulent call would not have been made had it been subject to billing, if that call goes to an international destination or to a premium rate service, the operator on whose network the call has originated must make an out payment to the service provider or operator who carries or receives the call at the distant end. As fraud patterns are essentially a reflection of charging patterns (in other words most fraud goes to expensive destinations or services) a high proportion of all fraudulent calls will invariably result in such an out payment to another operator. When handling objections, fraud managers should point to this simple observation that at least 40 or 50 per cent of the value of bills written off is paid out by the operator while no corresponding payment is ever received from a subscriber. In networks functioning in countries that face foreign exchange shortages this is an even more significant problem as the out payments are generally made in hard currency.

In the same fashion, it can be stated that fraudulent calls for which no payments are received from subscribers must still be carried, in a technical sense, by the network and therefore a percentage of network infrastructure exists purely for the purpose of transporting this traffic. In networks where levels of fraud exceed one or two percentage points this means that substantial investments in network infrastructure, often amounting to many millions of dollars, are being made to carry traffic for which the operator will never collect a payment. There are also costs arising from lost opportunities to sell services to those who become the clients of fraudulent providers.

Additionally, some operators have even faced the challenge of congestion on their international circuits when fraud is rampant. Though infrequent, this problem is far from rare and the fact that fraudulent traffic can occupy sufficient bandwidth to deny legitimate subscribers the opportunity to make long-distance calls, while difficult to measure, is certainly important.

When fraud occurs, the operator will often be forced to take legal action either to prosecute the fraudsters or to recover debts. Over the years there have been some prominent cases many of which involved PABX fraud. In these cases PABX systems belonging to major corporations were hacked and attacked by fraudsters via the telephone network. Calls to expensive destinations were then made through the PABX by the fraudsters and these eventually found their

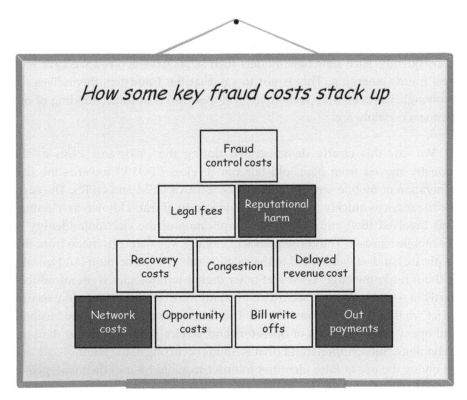

Figure 1.3   How fraud costs stack up

way onto the corporate customer's bill. In their efforts to escape excessive bills running into millions of dollars, those corporations often took legal action or faced legal action by the operator, all of which added up to reputational harm for both parties and significant legal costs.

Finally, each fraud case requires the operator to invest in recovery (investigations, collections activities, recycling of billing, etc.) as well as future fraud control initiatives to close whatever new loophole was exploited. Thus, even when most fraud has been eliminated, the ongoing cost of fraud control is a continuing drain on the operator and a potential inhibitor to the development and launch of new services. Figure 1.3, on the previous page, illustrates most of the components of the actual cost of fraud.

The Evolution of Communications Fraud

Fraud has evolved and continues to evolve. There is in effect a form of cascade whereby the introduction of new technologies triggers the creation of new services and this in turn demands that business models and operating processes also evolve. As we have seen, the shape of fraud is a reflection of the shape of the business in terms of commercial models, pricing models and billing models. Consequently, each time new models such as 3G have evolved we have seen new frauds emerging. This is not to say that the fraudsters themselves are evolving! However, their techniques and their levels of understanding of our business certainly are.

We saw this clearly demonstrated during the 1980s and 1990s as the industry moved from plain old telecom services ('POTS') towards the first generation of mobile services and thence towards GSM and GPRS. The early mobile services quickly fell victim to a new form of fraud known as 'cloning'. This involved theft and subsequent duplication of the electronic identity of the mobile handset. The consequence of cloning was that calls made from this duplicate handset were billed to the original subscriber's account but typically without his knowledge. GSM and other digital technologies were introduced partly in response to these security issues and were considered far more secure. What we then observed was that the fraudsters started to attack the business and operational processes of operators and service providers rather than the technology. Subscription fraud (that is frauds occurring at the point-of-sale and involving the use of false identities in order to avoid billing) then emerged as the main fraud issue for these networks.

This process of evolution has continued to the present day. Today's 'next-generation' 3G and 4G networks are particularly interesting because they are, in effect, convergent networks in which voice and data services are brought together using various radio and IP technologies and advanced roaming processes. They are also convergent in the sense that the service offerings supported by these new networks are a mix of entertainment and information related services, voice and data, and to a certain extent the claim is already being made that in the context of next-generation services the subscribers' SIM card is becoming a credit card that also supports financial transactions. The next-generation handset has been described as the subscriber's 'electronic wallet'.

If we wish to predict the type of attack that is likely to be seen in next generation networks, we must understand this pattern of evolution and convergence. This is simply because the convergence we describe above implies a corresponding convergence of attackers and techniques, meaning that hackers with an Internet orientation, telecom fraudsters with a voice call orientation and financial fraudsters with a credit card or banking services orientation, will all see fraud opportunities in the next-generation environment. Over time we can expect these attackers to transfer knowledge and skills and possibly even to collaborate with one another in subverting next-generation technologies and services. Possibly the first evidence of this is in the rise of mobile malware, wherein what was previously an issue confined to the Internet has now become a real concern for the mobile phone sector.

As with any form of crime risk, there are four initial points to consider when attempting to predict or investigate an event (see Figure 1.4 on the next page):

- *Means*: What physical, technical or intellectual means will the criminal require in order to perpetrate the offence? In the case of a telecom fraud this would normally relate to issues such as the technologies involved (how inherently secure they are) and the logical controls in place, such as encryption, access control, user restrictions and so forth, as well as the related business processes.

- *Motive*: Fraud may be committed for a number of reasons, not all of them financial in nature. Therefore, risk assessments that solely consider the potential financial gain for the criminal may miss critical issues. For example, a fraudster may be a disgruntled employee or ex-employee, whose motive is to damage the corporate

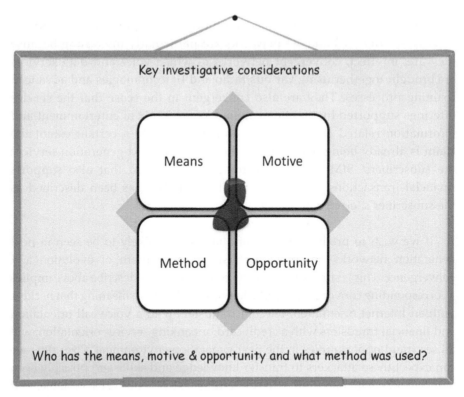

Figure 1.4   Key investigative considerations

image of the firm rather than to gain monetarily. Likewise, a hacker may wish to obtain free services in order to perpetrate an online attack free of charge while concealing his true identity.

- *Opportunity*: Historically, a great deal of telecom fraud was perpetrated or facilitated by employees or contractors, simply because the networks were relatively difficult for the average person to interact with and because the technologies used were not widely understood. In the age of IP, which now forms the backbone for most telecom operators, and of de-regulation we have both an open protocol, understood by tens of millions of people, and an open environment where almost anyone can enter the market in some shape or form. Hence we have seen the transformation of both the market and its fraud issues in a matter of just a few years.

- *Method*: Means, motive and opportunity will determine the methodology employed by the fraudster, but while it is methodologies that receive most attention from those interested in the subject, it is only a combined approach that involves detecting methods used while also addressing means, motive and opportunity that will ultimately reduce our collective exposure to fraud risks. Detection without risk mitigation leads to perpetual fraud that evolves little, while mitigation without timely detection leads to a rapidly changing series of fraud types that can leave an operator far behind in the race to secure its assets.

While effective communications fraud control requires an operator to possess the skills and tools necessary to gather and evaluate evidence in each of the above areas, it is the assessment of motive that is potentially the most fruitful but also the most challenging step; most fruitful because by understanding and addressing the motives for fraud we can eliminate some risks through re-engineering, but challenging because motives exist in the mind and may differ widely between individuals.

Nevertheless, where fraudsters have a clear commercial motive, a business case, operators have an opportunity to attack that business case intelligently, thus avoiding the need to investigate discrete fraud cases. Bypass fraud, described later, is perhaps the best example of such an opportunity.

Key Things to Remember

- Build a business case for fraud control

- Identify the true costs of fraud

- Each new technology can trigger a risk cascade

- New service models also create new fraud opportunities

- The fraudster also has a business case

- The best fraud defence may be to attack the fraudster's business model

The Impact of Mobile, Wi-Fi and Cloud Convergence

While estimates vary, our research indicates that there are now at least 4.5 billion active mobile devices worldwide (with new growth led by India and China) covering more than 60 per cent of the global population. Almost 50 per cent of Facebook's 900 million users access the site via mobile handsets or tablets (see www.facebook.com/press/info.php?statistics) while mobile internet access in general was adopted by half a billion consumers in 2009. More than 50 per cent of all mobile users now reject desktop computing for internet access altogether. In addition to social media take-up, which has been one of the main factors behind this rise, instant messaging, voice over IP services, multiplayer gaming, search engine usage, online banking and e-commerce are other key drivers for this growth.

Understanding, marketing to and managing the security of this growing 'mobile only' generation of users, sometimes described as 'the next billion users', is one of the main challenges facing mobile service providers, ISPs, banks, retailers, media outlets and anyone else providing goods or services in the modern world.

Other wireless technologies such as Wi-Fi and Bluetooth compound these challenges and we now see mobile devices connecting to the internet, or to corporate networks, via third party wireless networks that exist outside the span of control of corporate security. Indeed, our experience in this sector suggests that smartphone usage is also a major driver for Wi-Fi expansion.

Ubiquitous Wi-Fi coverage is now commonplace in most modern cities, and automatic searches for and connections to such networks are the default options for many users. As Figure 1.5 illustrates, this practice brings new risks with it as the Wi-Fi leg of the connection will often be via a network controlled by a third party whose security standards are unknown. This can expose users to 'man-in-the-middle attacks' which I also describe in more detail in a later chapter.

Cloud computing adds significant complexity to an already confusing picture. Cloud computing is internet-based computing, where shared IT platforms, typically remote, provide resources, software and data storage services to local computers and other devices on demand.

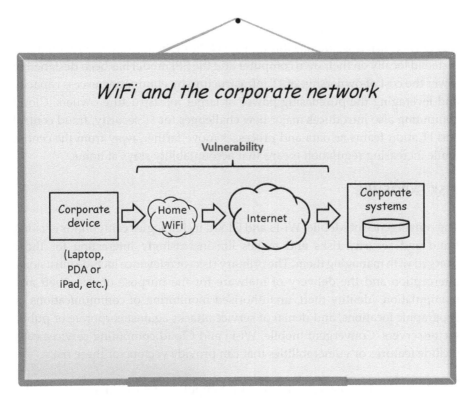

Figure 1.5   Wi-Fi vulnerability

The three service options in the conventional SPI model and their attendant features from a risk management perspective are:

- *Software as a Service (SaaS)* – in this model the software, platform and infrastructure are all managed for the user by the cloud service provider.

- *Platform as a Service (PaaS)* – in this model user does not manage the cloud infrastructure (network, servers, OS, or storage) but controls some or all of the deployed applications.

- *Infrastructure as a Service (IaaS)* – the user does not manage the underlying cloud infrastructure, but does have control over operating systems, storage, deployed applications and Firewalls, etc.

The SaaS services frequently take the form of web-based tools or applications that users can access and use through a web browser as if they were programs installed locally on their own computer and the SPI model has been designed to lower the cost of ownership of IT infrastructure by eliminating excess capacity and leveraging the purchasing power of larger infrastructure owners. Cloud computing also introduces major new challenges for IT security, fraud control and IT audit teams as data and processes move farther away from the centre, while increasing regulation means that accountability stays at home.

RISK EXPOSURE

The convergence of Mobile, Wi-Fi and Cloud technologies compounds existing fraud and security risks and makes life increasingly interesting for those charged with managing them. The primary risks of relevance include intrusions, interception and the delivery of malware for the purpose of data theft and manipulation, identity theft, unauthorised monitoring of communications or geographic locations, and denial of service attacks against corporate or public sector servers. Convergent mobile, Wi-Fi and Cloud computing services each include features or vulnerabilities that can provide vectors for these risks.

Modern mobile devices are powerful computing devices in their own right. The mobile user is therefore now a system administrator and this is especially true when a device such as a tablet or PDA is used on the move, in the home and also on the corporate or government network. The rise of the 'App', a low cost, readily available software application that may offer anything from productivity improvements to games, combined with the potential role of occasional child users and other family members at home, means that the introduction of malware to a mobile device is more likely than ever before.

Take-up of mobile anti-virus and other security applications is still very low and the vast majority of our clients report that they have no such protection on their mobile devices at a corporate level. Private users rarely have mobile anti-virus in place. When one considers the categories of information held on a modern mobile device (contact lists, calendars, email messages, user names and passwords, location service data, browsing habits, photographic records and much more) the risks of data exposure via extraction or key stroke logging are readily apparent.

Basic user awareness is therefore a key concern. Even simple errors, such as naming a device with the user's full name (as in 'John Smith's iPhone') and then leaving the Personal Hotspot active, can allow a stranger with their own Wi-Fi enabled device to deduce the name of a passerby when that network name appears temporarily on their display. Social engineering exploits may follow, either face-to-face or via social media and other means.

Wireless technologies such as Wi-Fi exhibit several important vulnerabilities, the most important being a lack of password controls or the selection of weak password, and the scope for the 'man-in-the-middle' attack, whereby a fake Wi-Fi zone is setup to capture user names, passwords and traffic by posing as the user's normal Wi-Fi service.

The main culprit for poor password security is the home Wi-Fi network. Again, the network name selected can be a key weakness, potentially revealing an address to a would-be attacker, or providing a basis for guessing a password. For example, an attacker may search for named Wi-Fi networks on a residential street, pick up a network with a person's full name, and then use online searches through sites such as 192.com and Facebook to gather more personal data on the target, including the names of family members, age, electoral roll information, photographs and much more.

In an industry that was once very concerned about the threat of 'dumpster diving' (searching through rubbish bins for personal or corporate secrets) any failure to focus on the risks inherent in Wi-Fi usage would be inexcusable.

Fraud risk managers can also expect to see increasingly frequent references to Cloud risks as they deliver their projects in the next 2–3 years and this will trigger a number of risk and security challenges. As explained, Cloud computing presents organisations with a complex set of options and the Software/Platform/Infrastructure (SPI) Cloud deployment model will demand informed decisions around what to deploy, how and where. These must be based on both a cost/benefits analysis and a risk assessment which should include advanced data classification modeling: what is the value of the data or the criticality of the processes and systems we propose to deploy in the Cloud, and what is the impact of exposure, loss of data or loss of access to services over various time periods?

Any estimate of the risks associated with exposure of data placed in the Cloud should take into account the following list of considerations, which are further summarised in Figure 1.6.

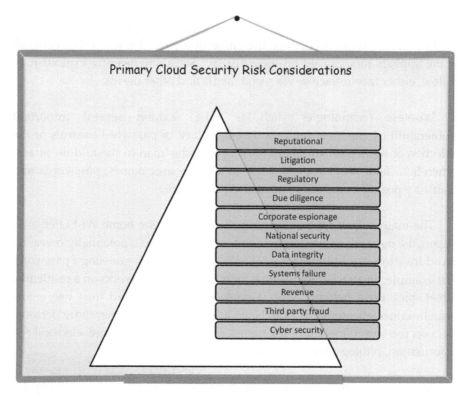

Figure 1.6   Key cloud security risk considerations

- Reputational risks or brand damage from data exposure

- Litigation risks and financial liability

- Regulatory risks such as those covered by data protection legislation

- Due diligence requirements

- Corporate espionage risks

- National security risks (particularly for the defence sector)

- Data integrity, completeness and accuracy risks

- Communication network and systems failure risks involving remote servers

- Revenue risks associated with service provisioning failures

- Third party fraud risks, particularly those involving employees of the Cloud service provider

- Cyber security risks such as hacking and malware attacks on Cloud servers

Cloud security risk assessments should map the pathways through your Cloud infrastructure and applications and establish clearly the routes by which key data travels or operational processes are executed, in order to assess the potential technical or business (operational, commercial or legal) impact of intrusions, fraud, data loss or process failures on your organisation, stakeholders, customers and brand. The impact of loss of service, governance failures and regulatory breaches should also be assessed.

Cloud security risk assessments require you to go beyond the standard analysis of business needs, assets and controls to cover the corresponding needs, assets, controls, responsibilities and capabilities of *every* Cloud service provider *and each of their sub-contractors*.

In a Cloud context, risks and the responsibilities associated with the control of risks and the protection of key assets, cascade down from the subscribing organisation though every tier in the outsourced service provider model. The scope of risk management does not end, therefore, with the prime sub-contractor; risk control in the Cloud is an end-to-end process in the full meaning of the phrase.

THE FURTHER EFFECTS OF CONVERGENCE

This convergence of vulnerabilities suggests a likely convergence of attackers, with mobile, ICT, e-commerce, e-finance and social engineering fraudsters, malware developers, hackers and other threat actors all acquiring and engaging targets across this common set of technologies. A converged threat calls for a converged response and the prevention–detection–investigation–mitigation cycle of fraud risk control will require the following features or capabilities, illustrated in Figure 1.7:

- Fraud prevention and security

  - User awareness extending down to the families of corporate employees

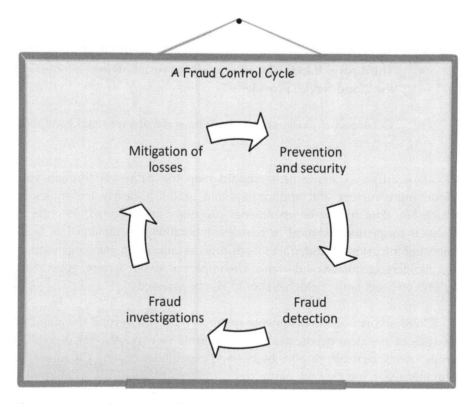

Figure 1.7   A fraud control cycle

- Network security protocols that encompass residential Wi-Fi and personal devices
- Guidelines on personal use, including social media best practice
- Mobile anti-malware applications
- Two or three factor authentication to reduce the risk of password exposure
- Encryption of data as a routine requirement, especially on portable devices
- Increased use of biometric security at device level
- Standards and auditing for an expanded set of third party providers

- Fraud detection

  - Improved surveillance of corporate network data
  - Monitoring of social media and other channels for reputational harm and new threat indicators

- Improved reporting by users of suspicious events, such as strange file attachments (i.e. using deep packet inspection techniques) or unexplained hardware performance issues
- Closer collaboration between Fraud Control, Network Security and IT Security

• Fraud investigations and mitigation

- Improved access to usage data and transactional data
- Enhanced AI tools for fraudulent pattern recognition
- Consolidated case management across corporate firms and sub-contracting third parties
- An enhanced focus on data protection during investigations that involve third party fraud teams
- Faster response times when the potential for brand damage is identified
- The development of social media incident response plans

In a nutshell, the convergence of mobile technologies, wireless networks and the Cloud means that we are witness to a shift to a model in which billions of potentially insecure computing devices, many holding sensitive data, will interface across millions of insecure or poorly managed private networks and access data or use services that are hosted in a virtualised setting and over which few risk and security teams have real control.

These changes dramatically increase the risks faced by organisations and their stakeholders, while they also increase the complexity of the fraud management task. Rather than making life easier, when it comes to fraud control, emergent communications and data processing technologies are making life more challenging than ever before and we will need to evolve our skills, processes and tools in order to stay ahead of the curve.

This convergence of technologies services business models and risks demands a converged response. It will no longer be sufficient for a fraud department to work in isolation and to focus on what it perceives as 'true fraud issues' while another team attempts to address hacking attacks and potentially a third team tries to deal with conventional mobile network and platform security issues. In the converged world, as we have seen, the attacker will make none of these distinctions and if we continue to operate in silo mode we will fail. We must now move rapidly to integrate the disparate teams working on these traditionally separate issues into a single Enterprise Risk Management structure which is organised and equipped to meet the converged threat.

The response to converging risks must also be supported by convergent applications capable of collecting data from the IP network, from firewalls and other security devices, from a multitude of service nodes and billing systems and also from convergent customer care and billing systems. These applications must then present this complex array of data to a user so as to present a real-world 360° view of customers and suspected fraudsters or other attackers.

The challenges to both vendors and operators in this convergent future are immense, yet at no time has this sector offered so much opportunity for a truly effective and holistic response to the range of threats it has faced throughout its lifetime. If operators can find the means to work together, and if the various departments responsible for protecting the operator's organisation and revenue streams can find the political will to share and to cooperate, then we have today the chance to build for the first time a genuinely effective and comprehensive set of solutions to a problem that has drained hundreds of millions, if not billions, of dollars of revenue annually from our organisations over many decades.

Key Things to Remember

- Wi-Fi networks are not always secure. If your employees use corporate devices such as laptops on public Wi-Fi networks, you may be exposed to additional cyber security risks.

- The Cloud has the potential to increase your risk profile and to make auditing more complex.

- Convergence also complicates the fraud picture and makes detection and management more challenging.

Risks in the Machine-to-Machine (M2M) Environment

The GSMA Fraud Forum has outlined the goals of the GSMA with respect to M2M services, as follows:

- Accelerate the adoption of wireless connectivity in wide range of devices across consumer electronics, healthcare, automotive and utilities sectors

- Meet a target for 2013 of enabling the market expansion to reach 500 million connected devices

APPLICATION EXAMPLES

Some of the applications cited, many of which already exist, are:

Automotive

- Auto insurance – monitoring of vehicle use

- Emergency/breakdown call – location-based monitoring to assist responders

- In-vehicle infotainment – streaming audio, video and online games

- Location services – information about local attractions and facilities

- e-Toll collection – automated motorway payments

- Fleet management and diagnostics – locations and condition of each fleet asset

- Stolen vehicle tracking – location, direction and speed of a stolen vehicle

Consumer Electronics

- e-Book readers – already popularised in the form of the Kindle

- Digital photo frame – remotely customisable photo content

- Connected digital cameras – instantly up loadable image content

- Handheld game consoles – streaming of online game content

- Personal navigation – GPS and other navigation systems

- Media players – streaming or downloadable content

Healthcare

- Fitness monitoring – remote monitoring of key stats

- Lifestyle and activity monitoring – monitoring of levels of activity and other stats

- Chronic illness monitoring – outpatient monitoring

- Heart monitoring – remote reporting of heart stats

Utilities

- Remote meter reading – for homes and businesses, without a visit

- Dynamic load balancing – instant reporting on demand and excess supply

- Remote system management – of power, gas, water and other facilities

THE ROLE OF ROBOTICS

Although the GSMA makes no specific reference to robotics, the rise in robotic systems is an obvious driver for M2M communications services. Many of us are unaware of just how quickly robotic systems are being adopted in many markets, and our knowledge of them is often restricted to those devices advertised for the home, such as the pet dog or automated vacuum cleaner, most of which are still viewed as gimmicks.

However, major buyers such as the Pentagon are not so sanguine:

> The Pentagon is spending £70 billion [$130 billion] on a programme to build heavily-armed robots for the battlefield in the hope that future wars will be fought without the loss of its soldiers' lives. The scheme, known as Future Combat Systems, is the largest military contract in American history and will help to drive the defence budget up by

*almost 20 per cent to just over £265 billion [$500 billion] in five years'
time. Much of the cash will be spent computerizing the military, but
the ultimate aim is to take members of the armed forces out of harm's
way. They would be replaced by robots capable of hunting and killing
America's enemies.*[1]

The remote controlled Predator drone and the numerous smaller hand-held
tactical drones, as well as the SWORDS bomb disposal machines (some now
fitted with sniper rifles and anti-tank missiles, in addition to their cameras) are
merely the first generation in what is intended to be an increasingly large and
important aspect of US military might:

- *Tanglefoot* is an unmanned vehicle that sneaks up on improvised
  explosive devices (IEDs) and very patriotically triggers the explosion

- The *Autonomous Platform Demonstrator (APD)* is an unmanned
  ground vehicle that can run at speeds of up to 50mph[2]

Communications links between robotic military platforms are already being
tested. Unmanned aircraft are communicating targeting information to APDs
on the ground, working in tandem to attack targets that cannot be easily
struck from the air, such as a lone insurgent in a crowded civilian area. 'This
system demonstrates not only the collaborative interoperability possible
among dissimilar vehicles, but also the numerous sensing technologies that
can be included onboard as interchangeable payloads', states Lora Weiss of the
Military Sensing and Analysis Center (SENSIAC) in her online blog.

So, robots are already talking to each other, potentially without any human
involvement in future conversations, and this pattern is certain to be repeated
within the civilian communications infrastructure.

RISKS ARISING FROM M2M COMMUNICATIONS

The communications risk management community has started to identify
possible security and fraud risks in these emerging models, with the traffic
light story we recounted at the outset being a prime example. There is already
a shortlist of concerns, most based on previous experience:

---

1   Francis Harris, 'Pentagon Prepares To Build $130bn Robot Army', *The Telegraph*, 16 February
    2005.
2   US Army, RDECOM.

- Theft and misuse of SIM cards (or equivalents) if these are not effectively locked down

- Decoding and onward distribution of downloaded content, breaching the digital rights of the producer

- Loss or deliberate disruption of communications links that prevents a remote service from operating at key moments

- Interception and decoding of location and usage data that allows unauthorised monitoring, for example, of the movements and lifestyle, or even the medical condition of a VIP or celebrity

- Other breaches of privacy and data protection through unauthorised access to the databases holding this new mobile data, with implications similar to those arising from the 2011 phone hacking scandal that brought down the *News of the World* newspaper in the UK

- While these new services remain in their infancy, it is already clear that this particular evolutionary step demands ever more sophisticated levels of security and control if operators are to protect the privacy and personal security of their customers

Conventional Communications Fraud Cases

DATA SERVICES FRAUDS AND CHALLENGES

As operators attempt to 'monetise' the bandwidth that many originally offered on an 'all you can eat' basis, they also face a small, but potentially growing number of data services fraud cases. A few of these involve direct attempts at theft of service or avoidance of payment targeted at the operator, while others focus more on attacking subscribers.

Nevertheless, when data services were first introduced by operators few anticipated serious fraud issues and the focus was almost exclusively on more traditional internet attacks such as hacking and malware. We have now learned a number of lessons about how some unscrupulous subscribers will abuse any loophole offered to maximise their usage.

Unreasonable Data Network Usage

When IP and data service offerings were still in their infancy, frauds on these services were limited in number and impact. Today 'unreasonable usage', often associated with illegal file sharing (see Figure 1.8), has become one of the most pressing issues facing data service providers, both fixed and mobile.

As telecom operators introduce new charging mechanisms for premium content and possiblymove to usage-based charging, we can expect to see data service fraud levels rise. As always, fraud follows the money and premium services have long been the main pull factor for organised fraudsters.

Almost every ISP and mobile data service provider will by now have a Fair Use Policy in place. In mobile networks, this is normally bi-directional, covering both excessive online activities by the consumer, as well as defining limits on roaming and similar charging by the operator.

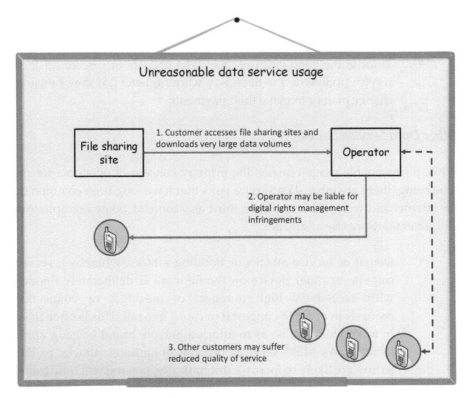

Figure 1.8   Unreasonable data service usage

However, unfair customer usage is becoming a huge problem for service providers and many operators are struggling to deal with a culture of excessive downloading that has become endemic among consumers. In one case we worked on, 20 per cent of mobile data usage on the network was attributed to less than 3 per cent of the data service user base.

Operators might face a double whammy as they could be held responsible by regulators for monitoring and preventing illegal consumer behaviour, particularly DRM breaches, in addition to finding themselves unable to recover the value of the excessive usage taking place.

The steps required to address this problem are not particularly complex, but they may be 'politically' challenging:

- Define excessive usage in the customer contract form

- Monitor usage to detect patterns that indicate illegal file sharing

- Forcibly move high users onto different tariff plans

- Throttle the bandwidth of suspected abusers or disconnect their service (following the necessary warning letters) if they refuse to change plan or to make their payments

Other Data Service Issues

While unreasonable usage remains the primary concern of operators for the time being, there are other data service risks that have long been common on the internet and with which operators must also contend. Some examples (we will cover malware elsewhere) are:

- Denial of service attacks or flooding attacks, whereby a server, cell site or other device on the network is deliberately flooded with excessively high numbers of messages or connection requests in order to congest it or cause it to fail. This is often done in a targeted way so as to attack a person, brand or geographic location. As M2M services become ubiquitous, attacks of this nature are likely to increase dramatically, making real time traffic monitoring at very granular levels an essential feature of network security.

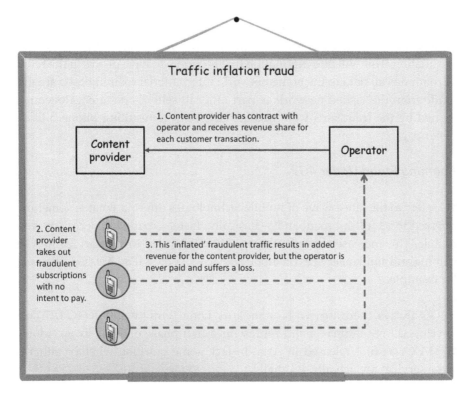

Figure 1.9   Traffic inflation fraud

- Content overbilling or traffic inflation frauds (see Figure 1.9) which can involve a third party provider deliberately overcharging for content or generating excessive traffic themselves, possible via subscription fraud, in order to inflate their revenues.

- Spam (typically via email but also by SMS, MMS or any other messaging channel) which can affect network performance and customer experience.

ROAMING FRAUD

Roaming Fraud and Call Selling

Roaming fraud has been a problem for mobile operators ever since roaming was introduced as a service option. Conventional roaming fraud requires fraudsters to first obtain one or more subscriptions from a mobile service provider. This is often achieved via subscription fraud in order to hide the fraudster's identity. One common practice has been to send the SIM cards obtained to an overseas destination. This will be a destination that is known to have delays in the return of roaming call data to the home network. International roaming calls are then made from the visited network as part of a call selling operation. Revenue is earned by the fraudsters from this activity, but the resulting phone bills are never paid.

Roaming Fraud Under 4G?

4G refers to the latest wave of mobile technologies offering what is sometimes referred to as 'ultra-broadband' – basically, faster broadband access on your mobile. This increased speed and capacity is intended to support 3D movies, gaming and similar services on mobile devices. Apple's iPad 3 is 4G LTE-ready, for example.

As always, there are two 4G standards. Long Term Evolution (4G LTE) was developed in Scandinavia and represents a first phase of 4G delivery. Mobile WiMAX was first released in Asia. In fact, some question whether either of these services are actually 4G at all.

Much of the fragmentation of 4G technologies is linked to a scarcity of spectrum worldwide. Spectrum has been allocated in different ways in different parts of the world over many decades and attempts to redress this have not succeeded. Spectrum is finite, while the desire to add new services is not, and this has led to a really difficult set of problems that will need to be addressed.

Although there are these compatibility challenges still to be overcome before 4G roaming will be effectively supported, as networks and services evolve, roaming is likely to become ever more seamless. Nevertheless, we can rest assured that fraudsters will continue to find the gaps in security and that roaming fraud in some shape or form will continue to be an issue.

International Revenue Share Fraud

IRSF cases occur when fraudsters employ various means to route traffic to 'audio-text' or premium rate services (PRS) that are actually located in other administrations. Callers are then charged very high rates for this traffic, none of which actually terminates in the intended network. The fraudsters receive a share of this international revenue from the PRS number provider.

This type of abuse has been growing in recent years and a range of techniques are used to obtain the ability to artificially 'inflate' traffic to these premium numbers:

- Social engineering

- Fake email instructions to technicians

- Voicemail hacking

- Teleconference bridge hacking

- Wireless identity theft

- Internal calling gateways

- Subscription fraud/identity fraud

This type of abuse has been largely associated with Pacific Island networks and the barring of targeted codes by other networks has significantly reduced interconnect revenue share fraud.

GSM Bypass Fraud

Grey routing, also known as 'bypass fraud', 'SIM Boxing' and 'Leaky PABX', has become one of the most widely discussed telecom risks in recent years. It particularly affects operators in developing markets where termination costs are higher.

The simplest way to explain this market is by way of an example (see Figure 1.10 on the following page). Here we consider a scenario where calls are routed from the UK to a developing market using a grey route.

A Grey Routing Scenario

The grey route utilises a VoIP PABX (Voice over IP Private Automated Branch Exchange) and attached SIM Box in the destination country, thus bypassing the conventional route and resulting in a loss of settlement revenue by the destination country.

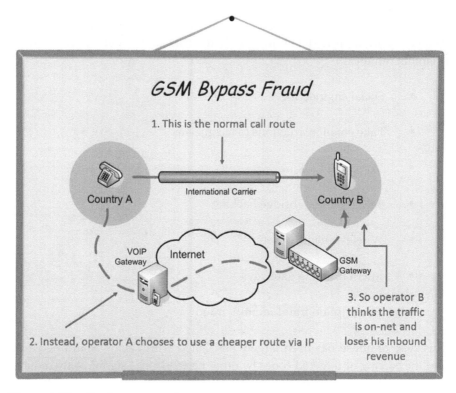

Figure 1.10   Basic grey routing structure

This use of a SIM Box or other equipment to bring the traffic back onto a local mobile network is normally the only illegality in the scenario although subscription fraud and other crimes have been known to accompany some grey routing cases.

The Main Actors

The typical supply chain runs from white and grey interconnect providers in destination countries with regulated (or relatively high market determined) termination costs to aggregators of international termination services often called 'carrier services', and then to providers of telephony and related services in originating countries. All companies mentioned below are fictitious – to protect the guilty!

EXAMPLE CUSTOMER

A mid-sized oil company *ABC Oil (ABC)* headquartered in the UK and generating a high volume of international traffic to their drilling rig, agents and suppliers in Country B.

SOURCE RETAILER

VOX UK – a supplier of telephony services to UK SME market. This includes mobile voice and data for ABC's UK workforce with managed VoIP PABX installations for multiple offices and leased data. The managed PABXs connect to Carrier Services UK to handle international calls.

WHOLESALER

Carrier Services UK has a soft switch set up with a Least Cost Routing (LCR) module. This selects the cheapest route on which to hand over incoming calls from VOX UK's VoIP PABX trunks in London. These routes have been bought from a variety of international carriers including a grey carrier in Country B – *Carrier Service Country B*.

GREY TERMINATOR

Carrier Service Country B is running a VoIP PABX connected to a SIM box with SIMs sourced from Operator 1 Country B. This is known only to them.

DESTINATION OPERATOR 1/WILLING VICTIM

Operator 1 in *Country B* has sold SIMs to *Carrier Service Country B* (who are operating under a different company name) and are seeing high volumes of traffic on the account which is always paid on time. This operator regards this as a high value business account.

DESTINATION OPERATOR 2/UNWILLING VICTIM

Operator 2 in Country B provides the corporate account for all ABC employees in the country. They have noted a lot of traffic coming to this account from a relatively small number of Operator 1 MSISDNs, although they can charge *Operator 1* for the termination of these.

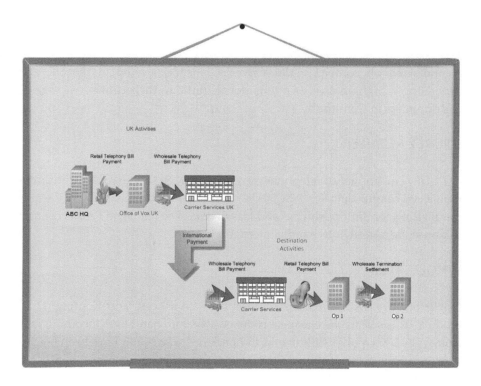

Figure 1.11   Flow of bill payments and settlements

Exchange Operators

Termination routes are sold in organised exchanges, through telephone deals to previous customers, and by arrangements on blogging sites and bulletin boards.

Both white and grey routes are sold openly and the grey routes are sometimes quoted as 'grey' or sometimes as 'non-CLI' routes. In both the formal marketplaces and the bulletin boards the QoS on the lines is often quoted, so an example of an actual quote is:

INDIA MOBILE WHITE CLI (919) 0.0101 45% ASR ACD 11+

where: CLI = Calling Line Identity

ASR = Answer Seizure Ration (quality statistic)

ACD = Average Call Duration (quality statistic)

So the above example is quoting the availability of minutes of termination to mobile networks on a white route to a region in India at a rate of 0.101/minute, with an answer ratio of 45 per cent and average call duration of greater than 11 minutes.

Technical Aspects

QUALITY OF SERVICE

Quality of Service (QoS) is important to the buyer of the termination minutes as it will reflect on them when they sell it on to their customers. The two most frequently quoted metrics are:

- Answer-Seizure Ratio (ASR) – call attempts answered/call attempts) a quality metric of the congestion on the line

- Average Call Duration (ACD) – an indicator of the voice quality on the line as the A and B parties will not continue if conversation is difficult and the ACD will be relatively low

Most CSPs will monitor these metrics to ensure good QoS is provided to their retail customers.

EQUIPMENT REQUIRED

The diagram on the following page (Figure 1.12) illustrates the main equipment requirements to provide a grey routing service. A Linux PC running open source PABX software with a SIM Box inserted as a card on the PC motherboard can be put together for circa $1,000 so the setup and operating cost for grey routing providers are very low. This is a primary reason why this problem has not yet been effectively addressed; the costs are very low while the rewards are very high.

Conclusion: Who Loses

In the above scenario, where calls were made on a VOX UK line and terminated on Operator 2's network in Country B (via a SIM Box on Operator 1's network), there are few actors with a real incentive to stamp out the practice.

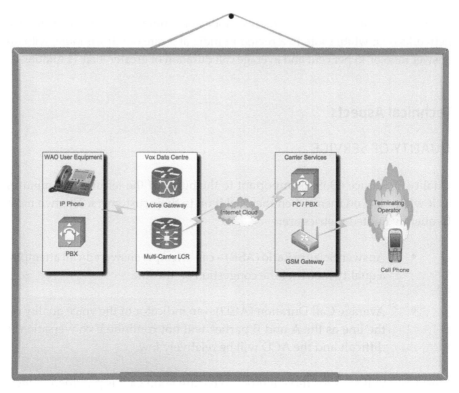

Figure 1.12   Grey routing equipment and infrastructure requirements

- ABC in the UK is happy as it saves a considerable amount over the basic BT rate to Country B.

- VOX UK is happy because it charges the customer the retail rate for the call (33.2p/min).

- Operator 1 in Country B is happy because it charges the local SIM Box owner for calls made on their device.

- Operator 2 in Country B is happy that they have incoming traffic from Operator 1 but disgruntled that they can only charge local and not international termination rates. However they may suspect that the alternative is for international calls to go via Skype.

- The national government in Country B (telecoms regulator) is the most unhappy as they can see a steady decrease in international termination minutes and the associated revenue to their exchequer.

According to the Communications Fraud Control Association (CFCA) $2.8 billion was lost to bypass fraud in 2011 although they do point out that this amount is lost revenue rather than the true cash cost. It's also worth noting that this figure represents only 0.0014 per cent of the $2.1 trillion of reported telecoms revenue over the same period, although some operators do experience much higher percentage losses. Nevertheless, with historical estimates of the cost of telecoms fraud running at between 2 and 3 per cent (CFCA and others), the impact of Bypass fraud may be less significant overall than some make out.

THE MAIN PREPAID SERVICE FRAUDS

Prepaid Top-up Fraud

This is primarily an internal fraud in most networks, although where credit card top-ups are allowed significant levels of payment card fraud have also been seen. This has actually been a concern since the introduction of pre-paid services with a credit card top-up capability. Stolen credit card numbers are often used to top up pre-paid accounts. The UK credit card industry reported a 25 per cent increase in annual card fraud losses following the introduction of pre-paid services a decade or more ago.

Prepaid Activation Frauds (HLR Tampering)

The most common prepaid fraud involves employees setting the status of a pre-paid account to post-paid in the HLR. The result is that the subscriber can make free calls because no lookup is made to check the balance on the account, as the system considers it a valid post-paid account.

These 'unmatched' billing records generally go into what is known as a 'suspense file' or an 'error bucket' when no corresponding post-paid account is found in billing system. In theory, these unbilled records are investigated and 'recycled' (re-billed) on a regular basis, but it is often the case that this does not happen, owing to the time pressures on employees, and some cases have been known to run for months or even years before they were detected.

One of the key challenges in such instances is to establish exactly who made the HLR change. Lax password security and sharing of user accounts is a frequent problem and tighter audit trails, regular reconciliations of the HLR tables against the billing system and prepaid platform, as well as thorough checking and re-processing of suspense, are all key controls that every mobile operator should adopt. This is one prime example of the need to consolidate IT Platform Security and Fraud Control (as well as Revenue Assurance) practices and controls.

Top-up Pin Frauds

When a customer buys a pre-paid top-up requiring the use of a PIN that is entered into the prepaid system via the handset, said PIN is compared to a table of active PINs within the system and validated. Once used, the PIN is flagged as such by the system to prevent re-use.

In real life, customers often experience problems with their top-up PINs. The top-up process may not have worked for some technical reason. A call to customer services can, in many networks, result in an employee manually accessing the table of PINs and resetting the status of the used PIN so that the top-up attempt can be repeated by the subscriber.

Of course, this ability to access and re-set PINs exposes the system to at least two kinds of abuse:

- Re-setting of used PINs so that they can be reused to fraudulently top up an account

- Viewing and theft of PINs, the use of which can be concealed by resetting them to their original unused status

Fraudulent Adjustments

Staff may also apply credits to selected accounts as a part of the standard customer relationship management (CRM) process. Such credits are generally used as a mechanism for redressing customer complaints. The business rules for the application of credits are often open to interpretation and a degree of subjectivity is unavoidable in many cases. This exposes operators to fraud by employees who apply credits to the accounts of friends, family and business connections in breach of the business rules.

Duplicate Voucher Printing

In some markets, voucher printing arrangements are surprisingly rudimentary and when top-up vouchers are printed, to be held as stock prior to being sold and used, there is always a risk that duplicate pre-paid vouchers may be accidentally or deliberately printed. If passed to fraudsters, the duplicated voucher numbers can be used to top up accounts before the legitimate versions are sold.

The impact in this is twofold:

- Fraudsters obtain free credit and can sell calls for cash

- Legitimate customers receive PINs that are already listed as used and then have to make complaints to customer care in order to seek redress

Scratch Card Tampering

Scratch cards that are manufactured in a sub-standard fashion may be subject to tampering that reveals the hidden PIN number, while leaving the card apparently intact. Again, this allows the PIN to be used while the card will later be sold on to an unsuspecting consumer. The impacts are the same as those listed above but in most markets the standards for scratch card manufacturing are such that this problem is no longer experienced.

THE MAIN POSTPAID SERVICES FRAUDS

Subscription Fraud

Subscription fraud (see Figure 1.13) involves the use of stolen or false identity information to set up telephone accounts with no intention of ever paying a bill. In the 'access' phase of this fraud, personal identification documents and information are stolen in order to obtain a connection to mobile services. This may involve theft of data from the operator's own IT systems.

Typical sources of stolen identity and personal information are:

- Internet investigations

- Theft of letters at the address

- Theft of data from operator or other business databases

- Social engineering via phone, mail, email or social media channels

- Malware (e.g. Spyware) on PCs and mobile devices

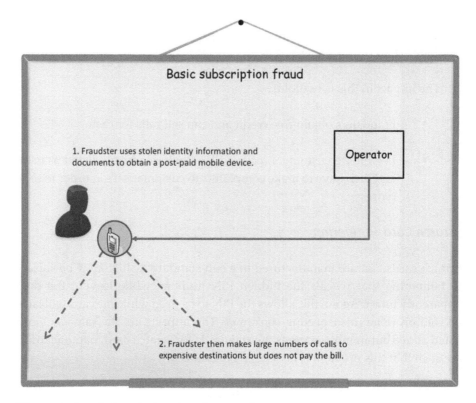

Figure 1.13   Subscription fraud example

In the 'exploitation' phase, the services obtained are used to generate traffic with no intention to pay. Roaming is often used because of the extended window of opportunity arising from the need for visited networks to relay call data back to the home network for each visiting subscriber. The primary defenses against subscription fraud include scrupulous adherence to best practice by employees at the point of sale.

Proxy Subscription Fraud

This occurs where a fraudster persuades another person with a good credit record to obtain service on their behalf. This is commonly done in exchange for a small payment and the proxy is often a student struggling with debt, or even a drug addict in need of a fix. Once the proxy returns with the new handset and SIM, the fraudster assumes possession and fraudulent traffic commences.

Test SIM Abuse

The use of test SIM cards by staff is another important fraud loophole. The problem lies not so much in the issuance of test SIMs, as in a failure to terminate their services once the testing period has ended. This should really be a simple automated feature, but in countless cases test SIMs have continued in use over periods of many years, often being handed down to friends and family by employees who no longer need them. The cumulative costs of this form of abuse can really mount upquite dramatically.

SMS Spam

Spam is the use of electronic messaging systems (email, SMS and Instant Messaging) to send unsolicited bulk messages indiscriminately. Spam is the electronic equivalent of direct mail. The barrier to entry is low, so 'spammers' are numerous, and the volume of unsolicited internet email has become very high.

The costs of spam, such as lost productivity, extra network capacity and fraud, are borne by the public, business, as well as by internet service providers (ISPs) and mobile telephone operators who have been forced to invest in spam filtering technologies.

Like internet spam, mobile SMS spam is a major annoyance for subscribers and impacts perceived quality of service. This problem is growing and some operators are introducing spam filtering technologies similar to those used by ISPs.

STAFF FRAUD

Staff fraud is one aspect of internal theft and involves the use of deception to steal funds, goods or services, as opposed to simple physical theft of goods or cash. Staff fraud can take several forms, including embezzlement, unauthorised credit adjustments, skimming frauds, data theft (e.g. misuse of online customer details, payment details and resale to competitors or criminals) and technical adjustments in the network to provide free services to selected callers or for specific call types.

Figures released by CIFAS, the UK's Fraud Prevention Service, showed that dishonest actions by employees to obtain benefits through theft and deception increased by 69 per cent in the year to June 2009 compared to the previous 12 months. Our own observations on projects worldwide lead us to believe that staff involvement (or, at least, gross negligence) probably accounts for between 50 per cent and 75 per cent of all communications fraud losses.

Editing of Free Call Lists

Most telephone switches include lists of numbers that can be called free of charge. Examples are the emergency services, the operator's customer services lines and others. It is often possible for staff with the required systems access rights to add numbers to these lists. Where controls are weak, these may include expensive overseas or premium rate numbers. Employees, or their friends and business associates, can then place calls to those numbers at no cost, potentially conducting traffic inflation frauds to PRS numbers.

Tariff Plan Manipulation

Billing of telecommunications services is a complex task. Not only must accounting information be accurately generated for all of the services consumed, but this information must also be collected, decoded, validated, filtered, aggregated, correlated, enriched and reformatted in preparation for distribution to each individual billing platform. Once a billing system has received this information the correct tariff must be identified, based on the service used and the subscriber's bundle, and then the published charges, including any discounts, must be correctly charged to the subscriber's account.

Even if all of the other elements of this process are 100 per cent accurate (which in our experience is unlikely), incomplete, inaccurate or out of date tariff definitions will result in incorrect pricing, resulting in either under or over billing. Worse, this could also result in deliberate exploitation of weaknesses in those tariff definitions by fraudsters.

These problems are not limited to post-paid billing systems; pre-paid billing, interconnect settlement and roaming clearing systems are also affected. In fact, all revenue streams that maintain an independent definition of tariffs are at risk. To complicate matters further, each billing system will have its own method of representing those tariffs.

So, what can go wrong with tariffs? Geoff Ibbett, of Revenue Risk Management Solutions, has provided six key questions that any operator should ask themselves in this regard:

- Do you know if all of your destinations are included in your tariff plan? If not, then you could be giving away free usage or be applying a low default rate.

- Do you know if all of your dial strings align with traffic classes? If not, then you will be charging incorrectly for terminating traffic to those destinations. If this problem is also found in your interconnect settlement system then other operators may see you as a cheap route to those destinations and are likely to be exploiting your generously discounted rate or deliberately avoiding using your network if your rate is higher than expected.

- Do you know if all of your destinations are associated with the correct rate bands? If not then the odds are that you will be under or over charging your customers.

- Do you know if your discounting schemes are defined correctly, in particular that promotions automatically expire when expected? If not, you may be unnecessarily subsidising service usage by your customers.

- Do you know if your active tariffs agree with your published tariffs? If not, then both under and over billing are possible.

- Do you know if your tariffs invite misuse because of differential pricing that can be exploited for the benefit of others? If so, your network may be subject to arbitrage or even fraud.

Many of these cases can also result in indirect costs, the main one being the handling of customer complaints which is likely to include adjusting bills and perhaps incurring penalties and rebates. It is also worth noting that over billing tends to be naturally self-limiting, as customers are more likely to complain if they notice they are being over charged rather than if they are being under charged. Under-charging, therefore, can potentially run on for long periods of time before it is reported and it is under-charging that represents the bigger risk. Overcharging often receives more attention from operators because of regulatory billing accuracy requirements.

Some of the symptoms that can indicate inherent problems with inaccurate tariff definitions include: reference data problems found during spot checks;

interconnect costs rise without an associated increase in revenues; increased traffic levels may be detected to specific destinations; transit traffic operating a low or negative margin; customers keeping to specific tariffs, or; a rise in arbitrage or re-file activity. There may also be increased fraudulent activity.

EXAMPLE

A telecoms company offered 50 free international minutes with any $15 pre-paid top-up. The issue here is that calls to international destinations incur termination costs and call sellers can use these free minutes to make money by calling certain international destinations (see Figure 1.14). This situation is exacerbated if those minutes are used to call the more expensive destinations. The operator receives no revenue for that traffic, wrongly believing that they are at least retaining a good pre-paid customer. At the same time, the operator must pay out monies to their carrier for taking the traffic. So, they receive no benefit of any kind but still incur a cost in this case.

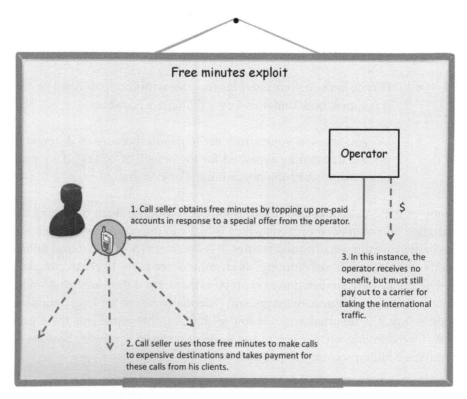

Figure 1.14   The free minutes exploit

Another common fault is where dial strings do not distinguish between different traffic classes, sometimes resulting in mobile traffic being terminated at much lower fixed-line rates. If this problem exists in the interconnect settlement system, then transit traffic to these destinations will not deliver the expected margin, in fact those services are likely to operate at a loss.

One recent project found that approximately 50 per cent of the billing complaints received by a European mobile related to tariff reference data issues. When their tariff definitions were audited, over 80 different tariff issues were identified. Based on their usage patterns, the cost to the company was estimated at around $10 million per year; purely because of inaccuracies in their tariff definitions.

This is where tariff assurance comes in: to protect revenues and costs by comparing published pricelists with tariff configuration data to identify over and under charging. This sounds simple but there are some complications, not least of which is the source of the tariff definitions itself. Often it can be difficult, if not impossible, to find a definition of the published tariffs in a form that is complete and up to date. It is of little value to simply reverse engineer the tariffs from an existing billing system. Rather, the price book must be compiled from source data that may be held in many different forms and distributed across the organisation. Finding this information is often the hardest part of tariff assurance.

Tariff structures must also be considered, including: cost bands (origination, destination, service class, direction, etc.); time bands (time of day, day of week, special days, start time, end time, etc.); rates (duration, volume, events, units, rounding, precision, setup fees, access charges, minimum and maximum charges, etc.); segments (stepped rates, tiered rates, multi-segments charging, etc.), discounts and promotions (event based, volume based, destination, bundles, account hierarchies, validity periods, etc.), bonuses (credit or discounts based on service usage, cross-product discounting, free usage, etc.) and the charged party (reverse charge, shared charging, revenue share, etc.). The way in which product offers are assembled from these tariff components is also critical to billing accuracy. Not only that, but this information is subject to constant change.

However, if this information can be obtained and codified then it lends itself to comparison with all billing systems on a periodic basis. Such comparisons can spot errors that result in under or over billing and provide an audit trail of the month-on-month changes being applied to the tariff definitions by the business.

A pro-active tariff assurance capability is therefore an essential part of any mature revenue risk management programme as it has the benefit of protecting revenues and reducing fraud and other costs that are extremely difficult, if not impossible to detect in other ways. It also increases customer satisfaction thereby reducing one of the three major contributors to churn and provides a company-wide reference data source that can support compliance activities.

Zombies (Deactivated in Billing but Still Active in HLR)

Cases in which subscriber's accounts have been terminated for non-payment, but where the service is repeatedly reactivated in the network are sometimes referred to as 'Zombies' – the communications industry's version of the living dead. Many of these cases result from the actions of a member of staff who is reactivating a friend's service whenever it is deactivated by billing and collections. Once again, the Zombie example underscores the relevance of IT platform security to fraud control.

Operator Services

Networks that provide operator assistance (generally the former PTTs or state-owned public telephone networks like BT or AT&T) face another internal challenge in the form of their operators. Operators are often privy to sensitive caller information (credit card calling, for example, was once very popular in North America) and they also have internal routes by which they can make free calls, as well as techniques that allow them to connect customers without triggering charging.

Operator services cases are today mainly confined to smaller networks, but as recently as ten years ago major cases involving hundreds of operators were still being reported.

THE MAIN FIXED LINE FRAUDS

Fixed line services are those traditional services we are familiar with, where a fixed wire runs into the house or office from a junction box on the street. Contrary to popular belief, fraud is not confined to mobile networks and fixed line fraud has a proud history going back to the earliest days of telecommunications.

YE OLDE FRAUDE CASE STUDY

As is often the case, what initially caused alarm bells to ring was a revenue assurance audit of the unbilled suspense files. As we will explain in more detail in the chapter on revenue assurance, suspense files are buckets of data records that have been rejected by various systems in the mediation and billing chain. In this instance, the call data records for several fixed line numbers were being rejected as un-billable because those numbers were not assigned to any customer in the billing system.

The case had some unique characteristics, which led the revenue assurance team to bring it the attention of my Fraud team:

- All of the discarded records, which amounted to $6 million worth of calls, were for incoming operator assisted calls from AT&T.
- Not one of the records could be linked to an instance of incorrect or delayed provisioning. In other words, none of the called numbers was in the process of being assigned, nor had any of them been recently assigned and then disconnected, as far as the service order record showed.
- None of the numbers involved was currently active in the exchanges; the calls appeared to have succeeded at the time (they all had durations) and yet not one of the lines was still in service when the investigation commenced.
- Finally, all of the calls had very long durations, typically of six hours or longer.

Looking at this from a fraud perspective, it took our team only a few hours to develop a theory. The most likely explanation seemed to be that an engineer in the exchange was activating numbers and then call forwarding them to working lines. This can be done without a physical line being connected to the active number, hence the absence of the service order that would be needed to get the actual wires provisioned.

Operator services collect calls, whereby the receiving party agrees to pay for the call, were then being made from the USA to the fraudulently activated numbers. Each of those calls was automatically forwarded (the standard warning tone also having been deactivated by the engineer) to the legitimate working line where the calls were answered and the charges accepted.

The person accepting the charges could then use call conferencing to connect the caller to any local number, secure in the knowledge that AT&T were unaware of the call forwarding leg, and would therefore prepare a statement that referred only to the unauthorised and unassigned called number. Thus, very large volumes of traffic were facilitated while all billing was avoided.

The fraudster clearly knew that the switch logs showing the identity of the person activating, editing and deactivating each line were being overwritten by the switch every two weeks. He also knew that reviews of billing suspense files were likely to be done within a month of the billing cycle. Consequently, he was changing the activated and forwarded number at least once a month, sometimes more frequently, to avoid detection through either of these means.

Armed only with this rather convoluted theory, we took the following steps:

- We started to capture all suspense file data containing call forwarded records on a daily basis in our fraud management systems. Analysis of this data quickly revealed a subset of calling AT&T numbers that were involved in more than 90 per cent of suspicious cases.
- We also arranged for a backup of the switch log files for every switch on the network to be secretly taken on a daily basis, with the assistance of a senior manager in network operations.

We asked the HR department to supply the personal file of every switch engineer and we built a small database containing name, address and contact number information. Monitoring of inbound traffic then allowed us to spot incoming collect calls from AT&T. We compiled a list of all such calls over a three-day period (these were only in the tens of thousands, so the data volume was relatively small), which we sorted by called number or 'B' number.

Next, we reconciled that B number list with a list of all assigned and working lines in the network. This left us with only a single B number that was receiving collect calls, but which was not listed as active in the network, according to the billing system.

Calling on our friendly network operations manager again, we were able to establish that this single B number (active in the exchange but not in billing) was currently forwarded to a working telephone line and that this line did indeed have the call conferencing feature assigned. Furthermore, the switch logs showed a user name and password belonging to a switch engineer we shall call Fred.

Taking the number to which the calls were being forwarded, and the address listed in billing for that number, we ran a further reconciliation against the employee name, address and contact phone number list we had created earlier, on the off chance that the culprit might have made a slip. He had. Our switch engineer Fred had written that exact address and phone number on his paper application for employment 15 years earlier!

With these major breakthroughs, we next visited the address in question, accompanied by the police, and there we found a young woman sitting by the phone and acting as a telephone operator. She appeared not to fully appreciate the impact of her actions and she readily gave us a signed statement naming Fred as her 'employer'. (Note, in the environment in question we were 'acting to collect a debt', and had some flexibility with respect to procedure.)

With the girl's statement, the call records, the switch logs and Fred's HR file, we then trooped up to the head of HR for another in a long string of disciplinary interviews. This one led to Fred's dismissal from the company and his conviction on fraud charges, but not a single penny of the $6 million was ever recovered.

We include the above case to underscore the lengths to which fraudsters often go and the challenging nature of some fraud investigations. It is worth noting that the case involved not one but several types of potentially fraudulent act:

- The unauthorised activation of the numbers used

- The provision of call forwarding and call conferencing without a service order

- The generation of the fraudulent traffic

- Conspiring with accomplices at both the distant end and local ends of the scheme to defraud the operator

- The collection of moneys for the services provided fraudulently at the point of origin

- Presumed avoidance of tax, national insurance contributions, etc.

- Possibly even money laundering offences, depending on how the proceeds of crime were remitted to the organiser

Fixed Line Bypass

This problem is identical to GSM Bypass, except that alternative technical methods (normally PABX based) are used to route IP traffic into the home network without it transiting the correct interconnect routes.

This approach is less prevalent than the GSM option because the equipment is less portable and therefore the risk of detection is greater.

PABX DISA Fraud

PABX (Private Automated Branch Exchange) fraud has long been one of the most significant fixed line frauds because of its impact on corporate clients and relative high profile individual cases have been known to cost millions of dollars.

The fraud is perpetrated by the unauthorised use of a feature on the PABX called 'DISA' (Direct Inward System Access). DISA was designed to allow employees of a corporation, for example, to make cheaper calls via their company systems when visiting a different city or country, rather than using mobile services of expensive hotel lines. In order to use the service, the employee dials an access number and enters a code. They are then given a dial tone and can make calls to anywhere via the PABX. The PABX owner (e.g. the employee's company) then pays the bill for those calls.

Fraudsters obtain the DISA code using hacking or social engineering methodologies, and then dial into the hacked PABX with a local call and out

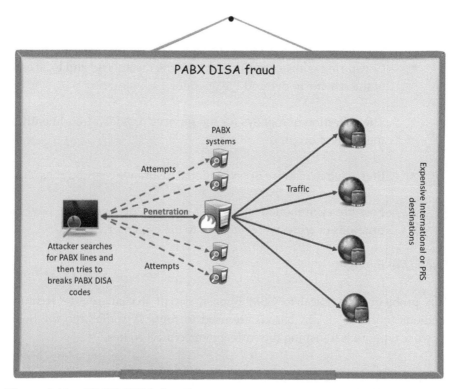

Figure 1.15   PABX DISA fraud

again to an international number (Figure 1.15). The fraudster can then set up large volumes of traffic through the PABX and sell calls cheaply to his own user base. The corporate client owning the PABX receives the bill for this extra traffic, as a part of their normal PABX bill.

Clip-on Fraud

One of the oldest forms of fixed line fraud, clip-on fraud involves the attachment of wires to fixed line cables in order to obtain dial tone. Calls are then made on the account of the legitimate fixed line subscriber, who receives the bill for the calls (see Figure 1.16).

This problem typically manifests itself in poor urban communities, especially at junction boxes in high rise buildings, or on the drop wires outside commercial premises. One of the most common targets is often a business that is closed over the weekends and at night.

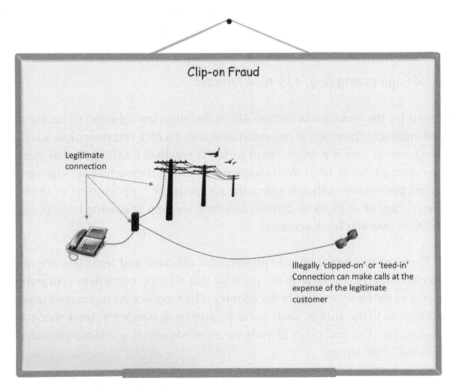

Figure 1.16   Clip-on fraud

Clip-on fraud needs to be investigated physically by tracing the customer's cable pair from the customer's premises back towards the exchange in order to detect evidence of tampering. This evidence may be difficult to spot as fraudsters will attempt to repair the damage done to the cables in order to conceal their activities.

COMMERCIAL FRAUDS

Some frauds are organised along the lines of a business venture. We refer to these wholesale frauds as Commercial Frauds.

Call-back Fraud ('Wangiri')

Wangiri fraud involves a computer using hundreds of connections to call random mobile phone numbers. The numbers show as missed calls on the recipient's handset. A percentage of customers will generally call back to see who called them. The numbers they call back are either premium rate lines with high charges, or they deliver advertising. Individual subscribers lose very small amounts of money, but the fraudsters can generate significant revenues if they achieve scale.

Social Engineering (e.g. 419-type Frauds)

Named for the violation of Section 419 of the Nigerian Criminal Code, the 419 scam combines the threat of impersonation fraud with a variation of an advance fee scheme in which a letter, email or fax is received by the potential victim. The communication from individuals representing themselves as Nigerian or foreign government officials offers the recipient the 'opportunity' to share in a percentage of millions of dollars, soliciting for help in placing large sums of money in overseas bank accounts.

Payment of taxes, bribes to government officials, and legal fees are often described in great detail with the promise that all expenses will be reimbursed as soon as the funds are out of the country. The recipient is encouraged to send information to the author, such as blank letterhead stationery, bank name and account numbers, and other identifying information using a facsimile number provided in the letter.

These schemes rely on convincing a willing victim to send money to the author of the letter in several installments of increasing amounts for a variety of reasons. To a certain extent, greed and the belief that one can sometimes get something for nothing, provide the psychological basis for the fraudster's exploit.[3]

Long Firm Fraud

Long firm 'fraud' involves fraudsters setting up what seems to be a legitimate business and running it over a long period of time in order to build up trust with suppliers and the bank, and a good credit rating. Once they have achieved this, they go for a series of 'big hits' and then vanish with the goods or funds received.

Long firm fraud requires operators to conduct due diligence on the firms that enter into business contracts for multiple lines or services:

- Who are the directors?

- Who are the beneficial owners?

- What business are they in?

- Is their business model credible?

- Does their model explain the type and volume of services they are ordering and their patterns of use?

As you can see, communications fraud is complex and each case may involve any combination of techniques. Each of the scenarios we go through in this text is only a potential building block for large and complex fraud cases. Investigators need to understand this and think laterally as they pursue their leads.

---

3   The Internet Crime Complaint Centre.

2

Revenue Assurance

With a major contribution by Geoff Ibbett of Revenue Risk Management Solutions

Defining Revenue Assurance

While fraud and security may seem sexy to some, the biggest area of revenue risk in the telecom sector doesn't arise from deliberate criminality, it results from errors. The practice that addresses this surprisingly long list of issues is known as 'Revenue Assurance' and over the past decade it has grown in importance and sophistication. If fraud sits under the stairs, revenue assurance lives in the garage, surrounded by a jumble of tools and old parts from this and that.

RA, as it is generally called, ideally operates in close collaboration with Fraud Risk Management, and my RA guru is Geoff Ibbett of Revenue Risk Management Solutions. I have worked closely with Geoff on a number of complex projects over several years, ruthlessly exploiting his extensive knowledge of RA risks and controls. A great part of the content of this chapter is based on the lessons he has taught me, or on the observations I have made while watching him work.

In order to understand the scope of RA it is necessary to start with a model. The collection and analysis of Telecom data for the purpose of validating the completeness, accuracy and timeliness of billing (Figure 2.1) is a challenging task that requires the simultaneous application of:

- Deep technical knowledge of telecoms infrastructures, multiple data sources and encoding formats

- Forensic data analysis skills to execute advanced reconciliations, filtering, service mapping and root cause analysis

- Financial accounting skills to review price plans, validate charging and billing processes, while also assuring charging accuracy at both macro and account levels

In modern telecoms firms, these activities must be performed across multiple technologies and services, including:

- Mobile, 3G and 4G

- Fixed

- Data, including mobile broadband, ultra broadband, etc.

- Internet

- Roaming

- Value added services

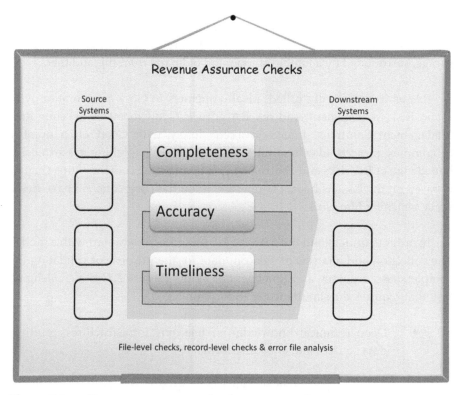

Figure 2.1   Revenue assurance checks

Table 2.1   Common leakage issues and key impacts

Common Issues	Key Business Impacts
Incomplete charging/billing	Revenue loss
Inaccurate charging/billing	Revenue loss of overcharging*
Late charging/billing	Cost of deferred revenue
Inefficient provisioning	Cost of resources
Delayed activations	Opportunity cost and churn
Excessive unbilled data usage	Cost of unprofitable capacity
Failure to comply with regulations	Penalties and brand damage

* Overcharging cases may also expose the operator to financial or other penalties imposed by the local regulatory body. They can also have a negative effect on the brand and customer loyalty.

Key RA Drivers

Revenue Assurance has at least two facets and the scope of RA operations reflects this. On the one hand, RA addresses financial losses and recoveries that are primarily of interest to the finance function and to management. However, as profitability and operational efficiency are targets for the entire business, the technical and operational aspects of RA analysis should be of great interest to network operations, IT, billing, fraud and even credit control.

These varied drivers translate into a set of activities that extend from end-to-end analysis of billing data to management and reconciliations between technical platforms. Examples of some common leakage issues and their impact on the business are shown in Table 2.1 above.

Revenue Assurance is complex, varied and evolving. Each type of operator has different models and priorities, and RA experts do not always agree on the scope of RA. Historically, RA was viewed as being primarily focused on the reconciliation of usage and charging records, end-to-end and between platforms in the billing chain, but it is now much broader in scope.

Structure

Modern RA has grown to cover a number of additional types of analysis, including billing, rating, tariffs, usage and cost assurance. A typical model is shown here, but be prepared to see other interpretations of the scope of RA as there are several different viewpoints.

BILLING ASSURANCE

The purpose of Billing Assurance is to ensure that tariffs, rates and prices for subscriptions or event-based offers are accurate and correspond to those published or contractually agreed.

Billing Assurance also validates the application of business rules for discounting and adjustments based on packages, bundles or customer segments. Billing Assurance validates the completeness and accuracy of billing processes, assuring that neither over- or under-billing are occurring, and that settlement statements between the operator and third parties (interconnect, roaming and value added services and content providers) are also accurate. Finally, Billing Assurance ensures that billing is being conducted in a timely fashion, primarily by addressing the issue of errors and recycling.

SUBSCRIPTION ASSURANCE

Also known as Configuration Assurance or Service Assurance (all names are correct), Subscription Assurance validates the integrity of data across core network systems that manage subscribers' service status. These include key network elements, provisioning, IN platforms and billing platforms.

This primarily involves the execution of data reconciliations between the data tables held in each platform, in order to identify mismatches, and the investigation of any exceptions found.

The goal of Subscription Assurance is to confirm that even where billing and other processes are accurate, services are not being provided to subscribers who are not entitled to them, and also that legitimate subscribers are not being denied services and features they should receive. Subscription Assurance therefore addresses both revenue leakage and opportunity costs.

USAGE ASSURANCE

Usage Assurance primarily involves the use of a combination of KPI reconciliation, trend analysis and detailed record-level comparisons to monitor the flow of billing data from a number of source systems through intermediate devices (such as Mediation and/or Rating) and into key downstream systems.

Examples of downstream systems include:

- Billing

- Settlement Billing

- Prepaid IN

- Data warehouse

- Fraud management

Usage Assurance processes are conducted independently of Billing and Subscription Assurance, and focus on the accuracy, processing and delivery of usage data both within an organisation and also between organisations. However, Usage Assurance does examine issues of data validity in the areas of duplicate records and missing or corrupted records or record fields.

COST ASSURANCE

Whereas Revenue Assurance focuses on the revenue management chain, Cost Assurance addresses underlying cost issues ranging from wasted infrastructure investments to reconciliations of pricing in contractual matters.

In recent years, Cost Assurance has emerged as a new facet, or extension, of Revenue Assurance, and practitioners and managers will inevitably come across this as a concept or an operational area within the businesses they engage with.

All products and services offered have an associated delivery and support cost. When revenue leakage or fraud occurs forgone revenue results, but operators still have to cover the cost of service delivery. In addition, payments to third parties for usage (roaming partners, interconnect partners and value added content providers) add to this cost.

PROCESS ASSURANCE

Process Assurance refers to the analysis of end-to-end business processes that have a lifecycle extending across several parts of the revenue management chain, such as the Interconnect Settlement Process.

It also relates to processes that are managed across multiple technical platforms, for example, the Rating, Charging and Billing Process. In such cases, a single process may be exposed to similar leakage risks (e.g. loss of data) at several points.

Mapping Revenue Assurance Controls

As there is a cascade of risks down the process chain, it is necessary to visualise the whole process in order to fully understand the nature and impact of each risk.

Revenue loss (often referred to as 'leakage') can occur at almost any point in the Telecom operation. There are two common ways in which to visualise this:

- By mapping against the Revenue Management Chain ('RMC')

- By mapping against the BSS and OSS topology (the physical and technical map of the network and its supporting business systems)

Leakage can occur all along the Revenue Management Chain. Different types of leakage (e.g. Rating Errors and Subscription Errors) often occur in various combinations at the same point in the chain.

No two RA reviews will be alike. You must be prepared to consider each assignment as a new intellectual challenge. Each Revenue Management Chain will have different specifics depending on the type of operator and the service types (e.g. post-paid vs. prepaid) so be prepared to design your own RMC to match the operation you are responsible for.

Leakage can also occur at most points in the network and BSS/OSS infrastructure. To a greater extent than the RMC view, the topological network view (Figure 2.2) will be very specific to each operator. This normally means sitting with expert staff to map out the view at an early stage, and obtaining a

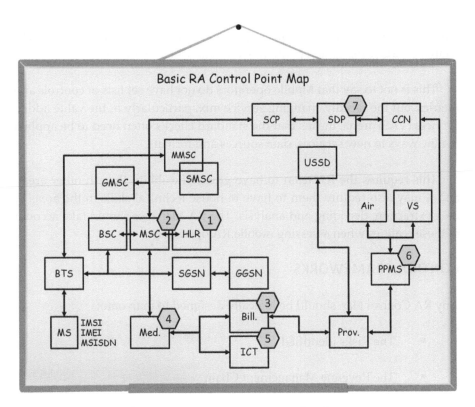

Figure 2.2   Mapping revenue assurance control points

briefing on the major services and key network components. If an RA operation is already in place, then the RA team will be able to map each control onto the relevant map. The diagram above provides an example, but a full RA topology map will be more complex.

At present, the population of platforms in these networks continues to grow, with each new service offering generally requiring a new platform (e.g. BlackBerry, Mobile Money, Voicemail, etc.). However, it is widely anticipated that more cost-effective technical strategies will be pursued in future, including consolidation of multiple value added service management systems onto fewer boxes, as well as the use of cloud computing and managed services outsourcing. Such changes might actually make the management task more complex.

INCREASING SERVICE COMPLEXITY

Due to the close-to-real-time nature of mobile operations, and the characteristics of prepaid charging and top-ups, revenue assurance operations in Mobile often tend to be more dynamic, requiring greater emphasis on 'chain-of-thought' analytics, rather than the repetition of an established set of controls.

This is not to say that Mobile operators do not have set lists of controls and metrics, but the rapidly changing service mix, particularly in the value added services (VAS) arena, means that the standard checks often need to be applied in new ways to new services, data sources and formats.

This requires the RA team to have greater flexibility than in other areas, and it may also require them to have in-house technical skills in the areas of data extraction, decoding and analysis. The RA Manager should take account of these realities when assessing mobile RA operations.

CONTROL FRAMEWORKS

Any RA Control Plan should be logically designed to map onto:

- The Risks identified

- The Revenue Management Chain

The plan must indicate the stage in the revenue management chain that it relates to, what the control does, and the frequency with which it is applied (see Table 2.2).

Most operators will have a more complex control structure, but the basic questions still apply. For example:

- What is the logic behind the structure?

- Is it based on a risk assessment?

- When was the last assessment done?

- Has the ROI for each control been assessed?

- Is the frequency setting optimal?

- Is there evidence that the control is being executed as shown?

- Is the control effective?

Table 2.2   Sample control framework

RMC	Control	Description	Frequency
Order to Activation	Control 01		Daily
	Control 02		Weekly
	Control 03		Weekly
Traffic Handling	Control 04		Daily
	Control 05		Monthly
	Control 06		Daily
	Control 07		Weekly
Charging	Control 08		Weekly
	Control 09		Daily
	Control 10		Monthly
Etc.	Control 11		Monthly

Key Revenue Assurance Issues

ORDER MANAGEMENT ISSUES

The most common order management issues are listed in Figure 2.3 on the next page and described in more detail in the sections that follow.

Changes in Product Not Charged

Some operators offer groups of products typically with different tariff options that subscribers are able to switch between depending on their current usage profile.

Switching between some products is free but some incur a charge.

EXAMPLE

A mobile operator offered a group of pre-paid products with different price plans that had data allowances and bundled texts and voice minutes. There were charges to switch between certain products.

However, the charging rules were set up incorrectly in the pre-paid self-service platform such that some product switching events remained charged.

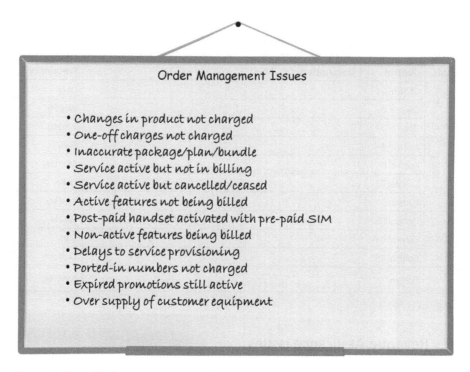

Figure 2.3   Order management issues

One-off Charges Not Charged

Products may include one-time charges in addition to the standard recurring monthly subscription fees and usage based charges.

Charging of these fees may also be subject to error and it is often harder to detect such under billing than it is with subscription and usage charges.

Examples include:

- Equipment charges

- Setup fees

- Installation fees

- Registration fees

- Transfer fees

- Early termination/cancellation fees

- Upgrade charges

- Change of tariff charges

- Call-out charges

Inaccurate Package/Plan/Bundle

Billing errors may occur because customers may be activated with the wrong package, plan or bundle.

In this case, the problem is with the accuracy of the order management process rather than with the rating and billing systems themselves.

Nevertheless, the customer receives charges that are not as expected and customer complaints, rebates and reworked orders are likely to result.

EXAMPLE

A mobile operator suffered from a series of data entry errors that resulted in customer orders being set up with the wrong product and consequently incorrect bills being issued.

Most, but interestingly not all, customers complained: bills were adjusted and orders were corrected. The main impact here was the costs involved in correcting the problems.

Service/Feature Active but Not in Billing

There are many cases of errors in the order management and service activation processes that give rise to the provision of service while billing will not be charging for that service or feature at all.

EXAMPLE

A mobile operator had a provisioning process that consisted of 12 separate stages. The early stages related to the activation of network services while the later stages related to the set-up of billing account information.

> However, the network activation requests were not rolled back if there was a subsequent failure in setting up the billing information, perhaps due to incomplete or inaccurate customer information. This resulted in a fully provisioned service that could be used, but with no ability to generate bills for those subscribers.

Service Active but Cancelled/Ceased

Just as errors can occur in the activation process they can also occur in the deactivation process. Two cases are possible.

Firstly, the billing account is correctly ceased but the network service is not terminated, resulting in under charging if the service continues to be used.

Secondly, the network service is terminated correctly but the subscriber continues to be billed, resulting in customer complaints for overcharging.

EXAMPLE

A fixed line operator received a termination request from a customer who was moving house. An error in the de-provisioning process resulted in the bills ceasing but the line remained active. The property was empty for some time, during which it was broken into, someone found the active line and started a call reselling operation to an international destination.

Post-Paid Handset Activated With Post-Paid SIM

Ensuring that handsets are activated on the correct tariff plans can avoid revenue loss.

EXAMPLE

In an attempt to reduce queues in its retail shops a mobile operator introduced an 'activate at home' service. Customers were able to buy a post-paid handset and SIM package and complete the order form from home and fax it through to the operator later. However, the handsets were not locked to post-paid SIMs and some customers found that the subsidised post-paid handsets worked with the same operator's pre-paid SIM only product. This resulted in handset subsidies not being recovered through the monthly contract fees as expected, thereby inflating the costs associated with that particular service.

Over Supply of Customer Equipment

Revenue Assurance is not just concerned with over and under billing. An increasingly important area of RA is identifying and driving down unnecessary costs.

EXAMPLE

A provider of fixed-line ADSL services shipped two ADSL routers instead of just one. They arrived in the same delivery indicating the issue was associated with the picking list supplied to the equipment warehouse. While the service was set up correctly and charging and billing was accurate, the operator was incurring unnecessary equipment costs for provision of that service.

NETWORK MANAGEMENT ISSUES

Summary List

- Missing CDRs

- Duplicate CDRs

- Incomplete CDRs

- Zero duration calls

- Incorrect number field formats

- Inaccurate timestamps

- Missing long duration record segments

- File gaps (missing files)

- Prepaid not triggering IN

- Unexpected routing prefixes

- Roaming, no contract

Missing CDRs

If the network does not generate CDRs for every usage event then billing cannot hope to be complete. Many scenarios exist where CDRs may not be generated by the network.

EXAMPLES

- CDR generation may not be configured for certain circuits
- Network elements may not generate event information at times of high load
- There may be a problem in the switch that prevents a usage record being written from its internal storage to a usage data file
- Not all usage data files may be transmitted to a mediation system
- If data is not collected frequently enough the switch may not have enough local storage resulting in files being overwritten before they are collected

---

Duplicate CDRs

Sometimes a network element may generate more than one usage record for the same event. If this cannot be detected then the customer is likely to receive multiple charges for the same event and be over-charged as a result.

EXAMPLES

- A network element may write the same usage record more than once to a usage data file
- A network element may write the same usage record to the end of one usage data file and again at the beginning of the next
- The same usage data file may be collected more than once by the mediation system

---

Incomplete CDRs

In this case CDRs are generated but there may be some information missing from the usage record or information may not be recorded in its entirety. If such missing or truncated information is critical to the billing process this will result in un-billable usage.

EXAMPLES

- Missing/truncated calling number
- Missing/truncated called number
- Missing/truncated subscriber identity
- Missing duration
- Missing timestamps
- Missing data volume
- Missing routing information

Please note that missing or incomplete information does not necessarily affect all billing processes in the same way. Just because it might render one billing system incapable of billing does not necessary mean it will affect all others.

Zero Duration Calls

A particular example of a network assurance issue is the recording of zero duration calls by network elements. In this case a real chargeable event has taken place but, for some reason, the duration has been recorded as zero. As zero duration calls are not normally charged, this typically results in under billing.

EXAMPLE

Due to a gateway switch configuration issue, a fixed line operator suffered from recording international transit traffic received from another operator with zero duration.

There was a mediation business rule that filtered out zero duration calls from the interconnect settlement system. The international traffic was routed and accounted for correctly on the outgoing gateway switch. Termination of this traffic was billed to the operator but no revenue was received from the originating network.

Incorrect Number Field Formats

When recording calling and called numbers within usage data records switches can use different number formats depending on the individual usage events themselves. If these recording anomalies are not dealt with adequately incorrect billing is likely to result.

EXAMPLE

A switch recorded most national calls with the national number prefix but a small number were recorded without. The billing system expected the national number prefix to be present and rejected those that were not in the correct format. Under billing was the result.

Inaccurate Timestamps

Usage records that do not contain accurate timestamps can result in the generation of incorrect charges in the rating and billing processes.

EXAMPLE

A switch suffered from clock drift such that its clock was running behind GMT by six minutes. This resulted in peak rates being applied six minutes late in the morning and off-peak rates being applied six minutes late in the evening. Based on the balance of traffic in the morning versus that in the afternoon, there was a net over charging of customers as a result of this problem.

Missing Long Duration Call Segments

Most networks can be configured to generate usage records during a call for those calls that exceed certain durations. For example, a network may generate usage records every 15 minutes. This means that a call of 40 minutes will generate three usage records: representing the first 15 minutes, the second 15 minutes and the final 10 minutes of the call.

These intermediate or partial records often need to be assembled into a single record for rating and billing purposes. If errors are encountered during this aggregation process often the whole call is rejected and will not be billed.

EXAMPLE

A network occasionally did not produce all intermediate records for long duration calls. In this case the mediation system rejected the whole call even though there was enough information to bill for part of the call.

File Gaps (Missing Files)

Billing accuracy will be compromised by interfaces between systems that do not protect against data loss due to mishandling of usage data files.

EXAMPLE

A mediation system did not correctly implement the native switch file transfer protocol employed and as a result did not collect all files from the switch. Eventually the switch ran out of storage space for these usage data files and when creating new usage data files it deleted the eldest uncollected file first.

The file collection protocol included the generation of contiguous file sequence numbers, but to compound the problem the mediation system did not check for gaps in this number sequence. Significant revenue loss was attributable to this problem.

Pre-Paid Not Triggering In

Network configuration errors can result in under charging due to incorrect service configuration information held within the network.

EXAMPLE

A mobile operator allowed its customers to transfer from pre-paid to post-paid subscriptions and vice versa. However, the provisioning process that performed the transition removed the customer from the post-paid billing system correctly but failed to mark the customer as pre-paid in the HLR.

This resulted in the MSC failing to trigger the pre-paid IN platform as it treated the customer as post-paid. While the post-billing system rejected the usage records because there was no longer a post-paid billing account for the customer. The customer was able to obtain free usage from the operator.

Unexpected Routing Prefixes

In this case the calling party or called party numbers have additional information prefixed to them. Such prefixes can render an event un-billable or alter the charges associated with the event; both under and over billing are possible.

EXAMPLE

A fixed line operator introduced an indirect access service, where customers could dial a four-digit carrier access code in order to select the long distance carrier they wanted to use for the call. These carrier access codes started with a 1, and are sometimes referred to as 1XXX services. However, the switch manufacturer should have placed the carrier access code in a separate field in the usage record, but left it on the front of the dialled digits resulting in these calls being charged as international calls to North America.

Roaming, No Agreement

Revenue loss is not limited to the retail billing processes. They can also be lost in other revenue streams, such as roaming clearing.

EXAMPLE

Audits in a number of operators have found inbound roamers from mobile networks that do not have a roaming agreement with the visited network. This is due to the base stations in the visited network allowing handsets to attach to the network even though a roaming agreement is not in place with the visiting network.

This results in lost revenues as well as inflated costs because: on the one hand, no retail revenues can be gathered through the roaming clearing process as there is no agreement; but, on the other, inbound roamers tend to make a higher proportion of off-net calls, to international destinations in particular, the interconnect charges of which will have to be paid by the visited network.

USAGE MANAGEMENT ISSUES

Summary List

- Incorrect record filtering
- Incorrect long call aggregation
- Incorrect handling of call status
- Incorrect call durations

- Duration rounding

- Incorrect routing of billing data

- Incorrect billing data processing

- Duplicate records

- Billing data not collected

- Roaming traffic not sent to clearing

Incorrect Record Filtering

An important function of the billing support systems is to ensure that non-billable data is removed from the billing chain. However, if the business rules that govern this function are incorrect then valuable billable data can be discarded.

EXAMPLE

A mobile operator needed to find a way to reduce the amount of data reaching its billing system. Their voicemail product was a good candidate as they did not charge for voicemail retrieval. The mediation system was updated to filter voicemail retrieval records based on the short code that was used to access the VMS.

However, the filter was implemented as a prefix match rather than an exact match; removing all calls that started with the voicemail prefix. This happened to correspond with an international destination and those billable calls were lost.

Incorrect Long Call Aggregation

Many networks will generate multiple usage records for long duration calls. If these partial or intermediate usage records are not assembled correctly into a single record for billing purposes then billable accuracy can be jeopardised.

EXAMPLE

A mediation system was responsible for aggregating long duration calls on behalf of the subscriber billing system. However, rather than accumulating the usage from all of the intermediate usage records it only sent the usage contained in the final segment of the call; resulting in significant under billing of long duration calls.

This was compounded when long calls were made to VAS numbers, as the correct out-payment was made, but the corresponding subscriber charge was under-billed.

Incorrect Handling of Call Status

To distinguish between subscriber-terminated and network-terminated calls, network elements will often include the cause of termination of a call in a usage record. If this information is not interpreted correctly billing errors will result.

EXAMPLE

A mobile operator did not charge for network terminated calls. They assumed a network fault had occurred and their customer services policy did not allow charging for such calls. However, usage records were also tagged as network terminated when signal was lost due to the subscriber's behaviour, for example walking into a lift or driving into a tunnel. Significant revenues were discarded until the business rule was adjusted to include these calls for billing.

Incorrect Call Duration

Network elements often record duration in units of seconds, but the way that they encode this information can vary. If this data is not decoded correctly, the billing system will receive incorrect call durations, resulting in either under or over billing.

Example

A network element recorded call duration as minutes and seconds rather than just seconds. The exact format was six digits in the form: 'mmmmss'; giving four digits for the minutes and two digits for seconds. So, a call duration of 130 seconds would be recorded as 000210. However, the mediation system regarded the duration as seconds, and passed the duration directly to the billing system causing it to overcharge customers for all calls longer than one minute.

Duration Rounding

Network elements typically record call durations to fractions of a second; tenths or even hundredths of a second. If call rounding rules are not implemented correctly, rounding errors can add up to significant unbilled revenues.

EXAMPLE

A mediation system was expected to round call durations up or down to the nearest second. However, it actually truncated the fractional part of the duration, so in effect always rounded down. On average, this meant that 50 per cent of calls were under-charged by one second. With per second billing and large call volumes this relatively small effect on billing accuracy can grow to a significant amount of unbilled revenue.

Incorrect Routing of Billing Data

Among other things, mediation systems are expected to deliver the correct subset of usage data to each billing system. If this process is not correct then billing will not receive all of the billable data that it should.

EXAMPLE

Identification of the data to be delivered to an interconnect settlement system was determined by which incoming and outgoing routes traffic had used in the network. The mediation system only sent usage data to the interconnect system that had used external routes. A reference table was used to differentiate between internal and external network routes. However, some new externals routes had been commissioned in the network without the reference table being updated in mediation. Consequently, some billable data was not sent to the interconnect settlement system.

Incorrect Billing Data Processing

Mediation systems implement many business rules that are applied to usage data as it flows from the network to the billing system themselves. Any errors in this process will cause billing inaccuracies.

EXAMPLE

A switch was delivered to the UK but not commissioned; it was subsequently shipped to Europe and entered service.

However, the clock was not altered from GMT to CET. To overcome this the mediation system added one hour to the timestamps of all usage records it processed. All was OK until daylight saving started, whereupon the clock was changed to local time, but the mediation processing rule was not altered. This meant that calls were charged at peak rate an hour early in the morning and charged at the off-peak an hour early in the afternoon; a net loss.

Duplicate Records

Mediation systems can implement mechanisms to detect duplicate records and remove them from the billing process. Otherwise, customers will be over charged. However, if the mediation system itself is responsible for duplicating data then billing integrity may suffer as a result.

EXAMPLE

A mediation system had a fault during decoding incoming usage data files that occasionally caused duplicate records to be sent to the billing systems. The usage data records was held in data blocks and in some circumstances the mediation system read beyond the end of the data block and decoded old data; data that it had already decoded.

Note that some billing systems are also able to detect and remove duplicated data prior to a billing run.

Billing Data Not Collected

The role of the mediation system is to ensure that all usage data generated by network elements is collected and delivered to the billing processes. Any data that remains uncollected will mean that the billing process is not complete.

EXAMPLE

During a period of switch upgrades, the mediation system temporarily stopped collecting data from each switch as it was being upgraded. When the switch upgrade had finished, the mediation system started to collect usage data again.

Except for one switch, where file collection was not re-enabled. A drop in billing data was noticed during the monthly billing run because data had not been collected for 30 days. The switch did store uncollected usage data but had limited storage. In fact, over 20 days of usage data were lost from this switch due to this problem.

Roaming Traffic Not Sent To Clearing

Mediation systems are normally responsible for delivering usage data to the roaming clearing system for inbound roamers. If the identification of roaming data is incorrect the integrity of this process will be compromised.

EXAMPLE

A mobile network expected its mediation system to identify and route inbound roaming traffic to its roaming clearing system. This process was governed by a lookup table of the network identities with whom the operator had roaming agreements.

A new agreement had been signed and the network had been updated to allow subscribers from the new roaming partner to use their network. However, the lookup table had not been updated and the mediation system discarded usage from all subscribers of the new roaming partner.

RATING AND BILLING ISSUES

Summary List

- Prepaid allowed with zero balance

- PRS not linked to billing accounts

- Incorrect identification of service

- Incorrect international zone

- Incorrect bundle pricing

- Incorrect tariff definitions

- Incorrect discounting rules

- Incorrect credits

- Excessive credits

- Excessive data service usage

Pre-Paid Allowed With Zero Balance

With pre-paid services heavy reliance is placed upon the accuracy of the online pricing and charging function. Any errors in its implementation will directly affect billing accuracy.

EXAMPLE

A mobile operator provided pre-paid services but the logic in the pre-paid platform allowed certain customers to make calls when their credit had been exhausted. This issue effectively gave free calls to those customers.

A related issue occurs where calls are not terminated when a subscriber's balance reaches zero.

PRS Not Linked to Billing Accounts

Billing issues affect all service types, including the charging and account of premium rate services. Premium rate numbers are non-geographic numbers linked to the billing account of the service number owner by their normal fixed line number.

EXAMPLE

A fixed line operator provided premium rate services (PRS) which were charged at higher rates than normal calls and a proportion of these revenues were shared with the service number owner. Some of the premium rate numbers were not linked to the associated billing account of the service number owner. Consequently subscriber charging could not be determined, resulting in no charges for these calls. However, the revenue share calculations were calculated correctly by a separate out-payments system, resulting in negative margins for those particular PRS numbers.

Incorrect Identification of Service

Problems with identification of service can result in an incorrect tariff being applied, resulting in either under or over billing. These issues often stem from an incomplete or inaccurate number plan from which destinations are to be determined.

EXAMPLE

A European mobile operator provided premium rate short message services. They should have been charged at a higher rate than normal SMS. However, some of the premium SMS numbers were associated with standard rate rather than premium rate destinations. Consequently, SMS events to these destinations were charged at a lower rate.

Incorrect International Zone

Billing accuracy depends on many factors, one of which is the correctness of the tariff definitions from which the rating and billing process obtains its charging information. If this information is wrong then the billing process will suffer.

EXAMPLE

A European fixed line operator had incorrectly configured their tariff definitions to include a European country in a rest of world zone. The European zone was charged at a lower rate than the rest of world zones, resulting in a higher charge to the subscriber than should have been the case.

Incorrect Bundle Pricing

With the introduction of bundled minutes and data allowances additional billing errors can occur if the management of these bundles in not correct.

EXAMPLE

A mobile operator offers a range of packages with different numbers of bundled minutes based on the monthly plan the subscriber had chosen. However, the billing system did not accrue bundled minutes correctly and continued to apply the bundled tariff (free in this case) to usage beyond the included minutes allowance, thus providing free out of bundles minutes.

Related issues include the charging of minutes at the out-of-bundle rate even though the bundle has not been exhausted and calls to particular services such as voicemail minutes that should be in the bundle even though they are charged as out-of-bundle.

Incorrect Tariff Definitions

The accuracy of the rating and charging process is heavily dependent upon the reference data that supports these processes, in particular the tariff definitions themselves. If there are any errors with these definitions then billing errors are sure to result.

EXAMPLE

A mobile operator had incorrectly configured their tariff definitions such that some off-net destinations were charged at the same rate as on-net destinations. These off-net destinations should have been charged at a higher rate, resulting in under billing of these services. The rating and billing processes applied the pricing information correctly, based on the tariff definitions, but in this case the tariff definition itself was wrong.

Incorrect Discount Rules

Errors can occur with the application of discounting rules leading to under or over discounting, both of which affect billing accuracy.

EXAMPLE

A fixed line operator offered a corporate tariff that incorporated account hierarchies. The purpose of these account hierarchies was to allow discount levels to be determined at corporate level by rolling up the usage on all sub-accounts.

If the corporate discount level was achieved then the discount would apply to all sub-accounts even if individual sub-accounts had not achieved their local discount level. However, only one discount should have been applied. In this case, however, both local and corporate discounts were applied, giving the company a double discount and reducing the margins achieved from these customers.

Incorrect Credits

Credits and adjustments can apply to billing accounts for various reasons. If these are applied incorrectly then lower revenues will result. This can be compounded if credits are given automatically and there is a fault in the business logic associated with this process.

EXAMPLE

A mobile operator charged pre-paid subscribers for SMS events by debiting their account when the SMS was requested rather than when it was received successfully by the recipient. In order to avoid charging for undelivered SMSs the SMSC automatically credited pre-paid accounts upon receipt of a non-delivery message.

However, due to an error in interpreting the SMS acknowledgement message the SMSC applied the credit for both successful and unsuccessful SMS events, effectively providing SMS usage free of charge.

Excessive Credits

One of the reasons that adjustments may be applied to a billing account is as a result of a billing complaint and can be used as a method to reduce customer churn. However, abuse of such a customer services policy can results in margin reduction for the associated products.

EXAMPLE

The customer services department of an operator had objectives relating to improved customer retention. One element of the operator's strategy was to automatically authorise credits and refunds based on the nature of customer complaints.

An analysis of such rebates was conducted and it became clear that a small minority of subscribers were complaining month after month and receiving rebates. The conclusion was drawn that some subscribers would complain even if nothing was wrong in the expectation of receiving a rebate.

Excessive Data Service Usage

Most data products have a fair usage policy designed to limit the amount of data used by a subscriber in a given period of time. If that fair use policy is not enforced then there is no incentive for subscribers to reduce their data usage. This can increase data costs and may affect services to other subscribers.

EXAMPLE

A fixed line provider of ADSL broadband services provided services at fixed monthly fees with differing expectations of data volumes transmitted by its subscribers. However, because the operator did not bill by data volume they did not have the ability to implement their fair use policy. Consequently, some users significantly exceeded their data quota resulting in higher data costs and complaints from other users whose service was impacted by these users.

PARTNER MANAGEMENT ISSUES

Summary List

- Incorrect settlement rate tables

- Over-charging by interconnect partner

- Under-charging of interconnect partner

- Missing data in interconnect system

- Arbitrage

- Interconnect re-file traffic

- Traffic routing errors

- Incorrect processing of reseller traffic

- Inbound roaming TAP files rejected

- Double charging of pre-paid roaming

Incorrect Settlement Rate Tables

Issues with billing accuracy are not limited to subscriber billing processes. Any revenue stream that includes a billing component, such as interconnect settlement, is at risk.

EXAMPLE

A fixed line operator was found to be undercharging their interconnect partners for termination of local traffic due to an incorrect rate configured within their interconnect settlement system. The invoices had not been queried by the other operators. A correction invoice was issued when the problem was found, but was limited to the last six months. Errors older than six months were written off.

Over Charging of Interconnect Partner

Other operators can make errors when generating invoices for their interconnect partners. It is important therefore that all interconnect settlement invoices received from other operators are checked against their expected traffic volume.

EXAMPLE

For over 12 months an operator settled invoices from one of their interconnect partners, who due to an error in calculating call durations were over-charging them, because they were unable to cross-check the invoices they received.

This issue was not discovered until the local interconnect settlement system received usage records for outgoing traffic and was therefore able to predict the call volumes and estimated costs on settlement invoices received from all of their interconnect partners.

Under Charging of Interconnect Partner

Just as retail subscribers can be under charged or over charged due to revenue assurance issues so too can interconnect partners. If the interconnect settlement process exhibits errors then settlement invoices are likely to be incorrect.

EXAMPLE

Due to a problem with service identification the interconnect settlement system of a combined fixed-line and mobile operator misidentified fixed line traffic as mobile traffic and mobile traffic as fixed line traffic for one interconnect partner.

The operator terminated significantly more calls to mobile subscribers than to fixed-line subscribers and consequently there was a significant loss of revenues due to net undercharging of the interconnect partner concerned.

Missing Data in Interconnect System

If the interconnect settlement system does not receive or is not able to process all of the incoming and outgoing traffic correctly, incorrect settlement invoices will be produced.

EXAMPLE

A fixed line operator had a problem with generation of usage data on a switch for certain types of traffic. Usage records were generated with zero duration even though the start and end times were valid timestamps that represented the call that had taken place. However, there was a business rule in the interconnect settlement system that ignored zero duration calls, but it relied upon the accuracy of the duration field rather than recalculating the duration based on the start and end times. Significant under billing resulted in this case.

Arbitrage

Other operators can take advantage of errors or loopholes in implemented tariffs, especially if they do not agree with your published tariff. A sudden, unexpected shift of traffic to your network could indicate such a problem.

EXAMPLE

A fixed line operator offered rates for termination of traffic to international destinations. However, when setting up the rate tables the operator did not distinguish between fixed-line and mobile destinations for a certain country.

The result was that all traffic to that country was charged at fixed-line rates. In effect the operator was offering highly discounted mobile termination to that country. Traffic was deliberately routed to the operator to take advantage of the low mobile termination rate.

Interconnect Re-File Traffic

In some circumstances other operators can deliberately make traffic that is expensive to terminate look like traffic that is cheaper to terminate, thereby reducing their costs by reducing your revenues.

> **EXAMPLE**
>
> In North America traffic termination rates are governed by where the traffic originated. Traffic originated locally is often cheaper to terminate than long distance traffic. Operators are expected to route long distance originated traffic down different routes to locally originated traffic so they can be billed at different rates. However one operator was found to be routing long distance originated traffic down a local route. The originating number had been masked in order to hide the origin of the traffic. This denied the terminating operator full revenues to which they were entitled.

Traffic Routing Errors

Revenue assurance is equally concerned with eliminating unnecessary costs as well as under and over billing. Routing of traffic over high cost routes is a example of how an operator can incur unnecessarily inflated costs.

> **EXAMPLE**
>
> A mobile operator had negotiated preferential rates to four international destinations. However, upon inspecting off-net usage records it was found that traffic to these destinations was still being routed to the national operator at significantly higher rates. These static routing errors can easily be detected using basic traffic analysis techniques.

Incorrect Processing of Reseller Traffic

When services are provided by third parties any errors in the billing and settlement process can directly affect the revenue and profitability of other organisations; increasingly, such errors are no longer contained to the local network operator.

> **EXAMPLE**
>
> A fixed-line operator had a number of resellers who resold minutes from the host network via PBXs. The host network was responsible for providing a monthly settlement invoice to these resellers along with a series of reports and a set of usage records from which the resellers could bill their own customers.
>
> However, these items were produced from different systems and the invoices did not agree with the reports or with the usage records provided. Worse, none of them agreed with the reseller's own calling logging equipment.

Inbound Roaming Tap Files Rejected

The roaming clearing process can also be a source of lost revenues or inflated costs if errors are made in creating the TAP-out files relating to in-bound roaming traffic.

EXAMPLE

A mobile operator's roaming clearing house rejected all of its TAP-out files to roaming partners in a number of countries due to the fact that the wrong currency conversion rate was being used. The operator had to reprocess those files with the correct conversion rate. While no revenue was lost in this process the operator incurred additional costs in correcting and reprocessing those TAP-out files.

Double Charging of Pre-Paid Roaming

The roaming clearing process can be a source of lost revenues or inflated costs if errors are made in processing the TAP-in files relating to out-bound roaming traffic.

EXAMPLE

A mobile operator had recently introduced CAMEL roaming and found a problem with its charging for some pre-paid roaming services. Not all pre-paid roaming services used online charging via CAMEL. Some were charged directly from the TAP-in file upon receipt from the roaming clearing house. Except in some cases the traffic had already been deducted by the CAMEL service, resulting in double charging in these cases.

Revenue Assurance Controls

This section explores the role that controls can play in reducing the impact that revenue assurance issues can have on overall billing integrity.

There are four main considerations:

- How to target the controls

- What roles the controls play

- What types of control are available

- How to identify the controls required

To achieve this we will discuss a way of sub-dividing what is a complex area into manageable components, of mapping controls to the overall operational revenue assurance processes, understanding what type of controls are possible and how to target those controls.

As outlined earlier, Revenue Assurance can be divided into a number of domains, protecting different aspect of billing integrity:

- *Usage assurance* ensures that the accounting of service usage is complete and accurate

- *Subscription assurance* ensures that recurring charges are complete and accurate based on the products that have been purchased by subscribers

- *Rating and billing assurance* ensures that all pricing, discounting and charging is accurate

- *Cost assurance* ensures that inflated or unnecessary costs are identified and eliminated

- *Process assurance* addresses root cause analysis, primarily the process gaps that allow these issues to occur in the first place. It is primarily preventative

Different control techniques are typically employed within each RA domain. When considering controls it is also important to understand which part of the overall revenue assurance process the control contributes to. As Figure 2.4 illustrates, revenue assurance teams perform four fundamental activities:

1.   The *detection* of revenue assurance issues.

2.   The *investigation* of those issues to validate the issue and identify underlying problem as appropriate.

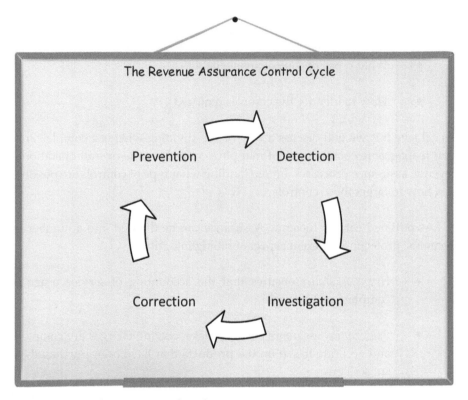

Figure 2.4   The RA control cycle
Source: Ibbett, 2011.

3.   The *correction* of issues that have been investigated. This may include recovery of historical revenue loss as well as resolving a problem for the future.

4.   The *prevention* of issues that may affect billing integrity. This involves proactive techniques and controls that can avoid a problem occurring in the first place.

Generally, controls are either detective or preventative in nature.

DETECTION

Revenue assurance detection controls have the following attributes:

- Control point (a data source)

- Control type

- Frequency (hourly, daily, monthly, etc.)

- Expected result

- Upper and lower threshold

- Alert

- Linked metrics/KPIs

These controls can be deployed in different ways in order to detect the existence of revenue assurance issues across all revenue assurance domains and lines of business, as outlined in the following table and explained in more detail below.

Table 2.3   RA leakage detection control types

	Control Type	Description
1	Metric comparison	Creation of a control total by applying a business rule to given control point and then compares it to an expected value.
2	Metric trend analysis	Generation of the same metric over time builds a history of values to which it can be compared. This provides the ability to detect values which are out of the norm.
3	Metric reconciliation	Comparison of the same metrics but generated from different control points. This is designed to detect discrepancies between control points.
4	Data reconciliation	Matching of data at the record level between two or more control points. This can identify missing or inconsistent data between systems that could affect billing integrity.
5	Call simulation	Identification of charging cases and comparison with switch call treatment tables. The purpose of this type of control is to identify charging cases that do not trigger usage records. It can also be used to detect incorrect network routing.
6	Balance control	Assessment of the accuracy of balance movements, typically for pre-paid charging. It compares opening and closing balances with related debit and credit transactions to ensure accurate charging of events.
7	Test call generation	Automatic generation of events within a network to a predetermined pattern to establish the accuracy of recording of usage data. It can also be used to assess rating accuracy in both pre-paid and post-paid environments.
8	Virtual CDRs	Creation of test CDRs that can be injected into the billing chain to establish the integrity of usage data management. It can also be used assess rating accuracy in post-paid environments.

Metric Comparison Controls create a summary control total based on the application of a business rule to a data source produced by a control point. That Metric is then compared with a fixed value. If the Metric agrees with the expected value the control passes, if not it fails and an alert should be generated.

An example of a Metric Comparison control is counting the number of files produced by a switch each day. If it is known that each switch produces a data file every hour then the Metric should equal 24 every day.

If however the Metric shows a different value then a problem has occurred and requires investigation. Some Metric Comparisons may include a tolerance around the expected value.

Metric Trend Controls create a history of summary control totals based on the application of a business rule to a data source produced by a control point. The current value of the Metric is compared with its historical trend and if it exceeds a certain tolerance is deemed to have failed and an alert should be generated.

For example, the number of records rejected by a billing system may be gradually increasing over time as general traffic volumes increase. However, if there is a sudden increase in rejected records it could indicate that a problem has occurred.

A number of statistical methods can be employed to generate the average, such as a moving average, arithmetic mean, etc. Metric Trend Controls are likely to have upper and lower thresholds associated with them.

Metric Reconciliation Controls produce summary control totals based on the application of a business rule to two or more control points that are expected to produce the same result. If the Metrics are within tolerance then the control is deemed to have passed, if not then it has failed and an alert should be generated for further investigation.

For example, if the volume of calls to a particular destination based on MSC records is greater than the same calculation performed on the IN pre-paid transaction log then a billing integrity issue could be the cause. Metric Reconciliation Controls are likely to have upper and lower thresholds associated with them. Thresholds can be expressed as a percentage variance or an absolute value.

Data Reconciliation Controls identify missing and mismatched data between multiple sources. They perform a record-by-record data match in order to detect missing and inconsistent data. It is often the primary technique for subscriber assurance controls where service configuration information must be matched and compared between the network, billing account and order information.

They can also be used as a diagnostic technique for usage assurance in order to identify missing usage records perhaps triggered by a discrepancy found with a Metric Reconciliation Control.

Call Simulation Controls compare known charging cases with switch number treatment rules to ensure that all charging cases result in the production of an event usage record. A script is run on the switch to dump the number treatment tables into a data file. The set of expected charging cases is produced by an analysis of the number plan.

Both data sets are fed into the call simulator, which then compares every combination of origin and destination and tests it against the switch number treatment rules. Any anomalies are identified and reported. Please note that call simulation does not actually generate any live calls; it is an analytical technique.

Balance Controls compare account opening and closing balances with the credit and debit transactions that have taken for the chosen accounts. This is typically used to validate balance movements for pre-paid accounts.

Open and closing balances for the chosen accounts must be provided, along with all credit and debit transactions that affect the account balance. The closing balance is predicted based on the opening balance adjusted by the aggregated credit and debit transactions for that account.

The predicted closing balance is compared with the actual closing balance to make sure it is accurate. If not then the control fails and an alert should be generated to trigger an investigation.

Test Call Generation Controls make real calls within the network to pre-determined destinations, at known times for a given duration, event count or data volume. Network CDRs can then be checked for completeness and accuracy, i.e. to make sure that CDRs can be found for all test calls and that they have the correct time stamps and duration/volume information.

For example, to protect pre-paid usage assurance test call generation could make calls from pre-paid handsets to check the production of CDRs on the MSC and a comparison with rated CDRs within the pre-paid IN transaction log. Some Test Call Generation systems include a rating component that can assist with rating and billing assurance.

Test Call Generation may already be used in your organisation for the purpose of regulatory compliance.

Virtual CDR Controls create event records as if they were generated within the network for the purposes of testing and validating the accuracy of post-paid billing chains. The actual event records created depend upon the tariff scenarios to be tested together with the expected billing results. The virtual CDRs are then injected into the front of the mediation system and traced to the billing system(s) concerned.

For example, concerns may be expressed about how call apportionment is implemented between time periods, in which case a series of CDRs can be created within different time bands and to straddle time periods to test the operation of the rating and pricing engine(s). This is a useful technique for post-paid rating and billing assurance.

Control Point Scoping

When considering RA controls it is important to understand the scope of the control. You won't be able to implement all controls in one go, so you should break your revenue assurance programme down into manageable projects based on the accepted risk profile of each of these areas. For example, you may decide that the rating and billing of your mobile, pre-paid, data services is your highest risk and prioritise accordingly.

Once you have defined the scope of the control and selected the type of control you would like to use you can then identify the control points that the control will operate on.

The control points for *Post-paid Usage Assurance* normally consist of:

- Network elements, primarily the switches (e.g. FSCs or MSCs)

- Mediation system

- Rating/billing engine

- A source of the invoices that have been issued

The data normally obtained from these devices is in the form of call detail records (CDRs). These records allow one or more end-to-end reconciliations to be performed. The detailed structure of each reconciliation will depend on which services are being examined.

The control points for *Pre-paid Usage Assurance* consist of:

- Network elements, primarily the switches (e.g. FSCs or MSCs) and other charging nodes (e.g. CCN for data services)

- The pre-paid IN platform

- Other sources of debit and credit events, such as voucher management systems and service platforms

The data normally obtained from these devices is again in the form of call detail records (CDRs).

The control points for *Roaming Assurance* normally consist of:

- Network elements, primarily the switches (e.g. FSCs or MSCs) and other charging nodes (e.g. CCN for data services)

- Mediation system

- Roaming clearing system

- TAP-in data files

- TAP-out data files

The data normally obtained from these devices is again in the form of call detail records (CDRs).

The control points for *Interconnect Assurance* consist of:

- Network elements, primarily the gateway switches (e.g. FSCs or MSCs) and other charging nodes (e.g. CCN for data services)

- Mediation system

- Interconnect settlement system

- A source of interconnect charges that have been have produced for other operators

- A source of interconnect charges received from other operators

The data normally obtained from these devices is again in the form of call detail records (CDRs).

The control points for *Wholesale Assurance* consist of:

- Network elements, primarily the switches (e.g. FSCs or MSCs) and other charging nodes (e.g. CCN for data services)

- Mediation system

- Wholesale billing system

- A representation of the wholesale invoices that have been issued

- The event information provided to the wholesaler

- Any reports that have been generated on behalf of the wholesaler

The data normally obtained from these devices is again in the form of call detail records (CDRs). The control points for *VAS/Content Assurance* consist of:

- Network elements, primarily the switches (e.g. FSCs or MSCs) and other charging nodes (e.g. CCN for data services)

- Mediation system

- Rating and billing engine

- A source of the invoices that have been issued

- A source of out-payment systems that have been made

The data sources from these devices is call detail records (CDRs). This allows one or more end-to-end reconciliations to be performed to protect VAS/content charging and associated out-payments depending upon the services that are within the scope of the project.

The control points for *Subscription Assurance* consist of:

- Network elements that contain service configuration information (e.g. FSCs, HLRs, etc.)

- Pre-paid IN platform

- Order information

- Billing account information

The data sources from these devices are normally service configuration information. This allows one or more end-to-end reconciliations to be performed to protect recurring charges for the provision of services depending upon the services that are within the scope of the project.

Subscription Assurance usually employs Data Reconciliation to detect service configuration discrepancies between the network and billing domains, whereas Metric Reconciliation is normally used for Usage Assurance with Data Reconciliation used to investigate specific discrepancies.

The control points for *Cost Assurance* should eliminate inflated costs as well as under and over billing. An operator's cost base directly affects margin and profitability.

This list outlines some controls that operators use to control costs as they relate to the revenue assurance process. They range from costs associated with equipment, unnecessary maintenance costs, traffic routing costs and costs associated with customer complaints:

- Equipment charges versus revenues

- Equipment rentals charges

- High equipment replacement rate

- Over-supply of customer premises equipment

- Circuit procurement vs. circuit re-sale

- Unused external circuits

- Overflow traffic

- Rebates and penalty payments

- Surcharges

- Commission payments

- Delayed installation costs

- Inflated maintenance costs

- Unnecessary call-outs

- Network versus inventory

The identification cost assurance control points is harder than for usage and subscription assurance mainly because the way in which these business processes are managed is less structured than the usage and subscription billing process. Indeed, you may find data source held in spreadsheets and Word documents, rather than in the more easily accessible structured formats.

Primary and Secondary Controls

When considering the operational costs of usage controls you may wish to identify Primary and Secondary Controls.

Primary Controls are controls that execute on a continuous basis and are primarily used to detect issues. They are usually end-to-end Metric Reconciliations, for example between network and billing.

Secondary Controls are controls that are useful to help investigate issues once they have been detected and consequently do not necessarily need to be operated on a continuous basis. If discrepancies are found then Secondary Controls, between inputs and outputs of individual systems as well as between systems, could help discover where in the billing chain the problem is located.

A risk management approach to the identification of controls is recommended. This is based on an assessment of the risks to which the billing chain is exposed and the impact of those risks on the organisation in terms of the completeness, accuracy and timeliness of the various charging processes.

Threats are assessed based on their likelihood of happening and the impact to the business if they did occur. Risk mitigation is achieved through the implementation of controls, whose purpose is to achieve a reduction in the risk to the organisation. However, it should be borne in mind that controls have a cost. A cost/benefit analysis exercise should always be performed to take into account the cost of implementing and operating each control versus the benefit to be gained from that control.

Other Revenue Assurance Issues

RATING ASSURANCE

Rating accuracy is a multi-faceted problem for Telecom operators, in terms of regulatory compliance, customer satisfaction, brand value and revenue leakage. Testing and validating rating accuracy is a key measure for revenue risk management, as well as corporate due diligence.

Implementing and assuring accurate rating is an increasingly complex challenge for operators. The introduction of a growing number of new services, from data to VAS, means that the number of interfaces and data sources present in the end-to-end billing process has also grown dramatically.

Consumers have more choice than ever before and accurate billing, based on accurate rating, is therefore an essential facet of every operator's business. A failure to ensure rating accuracy has the potential to damage the brand and reduce consumer confidence in the offering.

TARIFF ASSURANCE

Tariff reference data misalignments are one of the major causes of incorrect billing for most Telecom operators, accounting for as much as 50 per cent of all customer billing complaints.

Erroneous reference data costs money and invalid tariff reference data can lead to:

- Incorrect assignment of a destination

- Inaccurate rating of a call or event

- Incorrect discounting

- Non-expiry of promotional offers

- Inaccurate pricing of offers

Many other undesirable outcomes can also result. Ultimately these issues lead to revenue leakage, customer dissatisfaction, and potential regulatory breaches.

DATA SERVICE QUALITY SAMPLING

As operators move to monetise bandwidth, quality of service based charging will become increasingly prevalent. This requires managers to understand the service quality framework, as well as the mechanisms for measuring quality.

The quality paradigm is unique, in the sense that it is based on both scientific measurements *and* perceptions. If a consumer does not *feel* that quality has been delivered, then no amount of scientific data is likely to mollify him or her.

This requires operators to look at quality measurement from two perspectives:

- The internal technical perspective assessed though data sampling and testing

- The customer's perspective, assessed on the basis of customer experience and satisfaction measurements

Data sampling for data network quality of service verification (QoS) is still in its infancy in most networks, because QoS billing is not yet a mainstream approach and so billing accuracy is not affected.

Where operators do measure technical QoS on data services they normally get this information in Network Statistics, sourced from the GGSN and SGSN Nodes, Base Stations and IP Routers.

About the Contributor: Geoff Ibbett

Geoff Ibbett has many years' operational revenue management experience encompassing usage data management, revenue assurance and revenue risk management gained from both a vendor and operator perspective. He is a regular speaker at industry conferences and an active member of the TeleManagement Forum's revenue assurance initiatives.

3

Managing Communications Revenue Risks

Successful communications revenue risk management investigations require a mix of skills:

- An understanding of the technology involved

- An understanding of the services offered via those technologies

- An awareness of how customers are acquired, serviced and billed or charged

- The ability to creatively develop ideas about how revenue risks might be carried out or how leakage might occur

- The technical capacity to collect, read and forensically process the network, billing and financial data that could reveal evidence of a revenue risk

- The skills to question suspects and witnesses or to conduct audits

- The ability to present the findings of the investigation to senior managers, the police and the courts in a coherent way

- A solid grasp of the core principles of investigative and crime intelligence processes

- The ability to develop business cases or operational plans and to manage staff effectively

Few individuals will possess all of these talents, so effective revenue risk control starts with the recognition that a diverse team from a wide range of backgrounds and experiences is required. A team that is primarily technical is likely to find evidence of revenue risk, but unlikely to obtain confessions from suspects or to address root causes. A team that is too heavily weighted towards police-style investigations or financial audits will tend to spend much of its time chasing technically simple revenue risks that fall within its comfort zone. The challenge facing every revenue risk or RA manager is getting the balance just right.

In the sections that follow, we will attempt to use actual events to explain just a few of the ways in which communications revenue risk is manifested and controlled, while highlighting the importance of teamwork and collaboration, as well as detailed research and the investigative process.

Planning For Revenue Risk Control

Planning and preparation are as important in revenue risk control as they are in any other practice area. Simply by reviewing new services proposals, for example, and discussing potential risks along the service chain with the developers and managers responsible, most potential revenue risks can normally be identified and prevented. This proactive team-based approach to revenue risk control is the most cost-effective we know of and it certainly beats the reactive approach of detecting and investigating actual cases!

NEW PRODUCT RISK ASSESSMENTS

Here is a simple list of considerations for a product risk assessment. We use this list as a guide for assessing new products and services for revenue risk, but most of it is also relevant for reviews of existing products and services.

1.   *Knowledge of the Product Introduction Process*: Familiarity with the existing processes that operate within your business is a necessary precursor to actual participation in this process. Take the time to read existing process descriptions and to talk to experienced process owners before attempting to get involved.

2.   *Benchmarking*: Experience with other similar products and services will provide a good benchmark for the nature and impact of the

leakage risks likely to be associated with the new product or service. Checks with other Revenue Risk Management (RRM) teams and team members will frequently result in such references being discovered, making the evaluation process far less challenging.

3.   *Design for Billing and Subscription Risk Management*: Through the ongoing conduct of company-wide communication and awareness raising regarding revenue risk management issues, billing and subscription risk management should have been addressed by the original product or service designers. However, the RRM Analyst should be aware that in this industry there have been many instances of services being launched without any arrangements having been made to support billing. In other words, there is no such thing as a 'foolish question' when it comes to new product introduction assessments.

4.   *Risk Management Scenario Mapping and Testing*: Using the risk mapping approach, the assigned RRM analyst(s) should initially produce high level speculative risk scenarios for discussion with the process owners. Every attempt should be made to offer these scenarios in a positive and non-confrontational manner, as a mechanism for ensuring the success and profitability of the product or service in question.

5.   *Design Reviews and Adjustments*: Risk scenarios that are accepted as realistic, probable and potentially costly should lead to adaptations in the product or service design. These revised designs should again be subjected to a risk assessment to ensure that the risks previously identified have now been mitigated, no risks were missed in the initial analysis, and no new risks have been created.

6.   *Volumetric Projections and Systems Impact Analysis*: One common omission in many networks is the assessment of increases in data processing loads (e.g. xDRs flowing across the network) as a component of the risk equation. The Analyst should establish not only that provisions for billing these new types of service have been made, but also that the increased volume of data to be transmitted, stored and processed has been taken into account. This may require a review (and test) of the relevant business plan projections and discussions with network management, billing and IT, among

others. The most embarrassing example of such a problem that I have seen occurred when a fraud team signed off on a new service only to discover a few days after it launched that their own fraud system was unable to handle the additional data being produced!

7.   *Proactive KPI and Metric Definition*: A key output of this process must be the definition of relevant risk-related key performance indicators (KPIs) and related metrics to support the monitoring of the new product or service. Consequently, the Analyst assigned to the task must be capable of producing such recommendations and must also be well versed in the full range of existing and potential KPIs and metrics.

8.   *Live Product Testing*: As a final step before signing off any new product or service, the RRM team must conduct live tests to establish, as far as is reasonably possible, that the risk scenarios identified at various stages throughout this process have indeed been addressed. This testing may take the form of test call generation to validate rating and billing accuracy, penetration testing to validate platform security, or deliberate BSS and OSS misconfiguration (e.g. pre-paid set as post-paid) to validate business process integrity. Only then should the RRM team provide final sign-off for the new offering.

BRAINSTORMING

Risk Factor Brainstorming is a technique that supports collective decision making. It has been adapted from established approaches to decision making at other levels of management. What was once a consultancy-led boardroom process has now been adopted at all levels by many large organisations.

While strong leadership is often a good thing, as I have pointed out, communications risk control is a particularly complex and challenging topic and it is rare to find any one manager who truly understands the full scope of the risks and challenges. Involving a team of people with different skills, knowledge sets and capabilities is often the only way to devise workable revenue risk counter measures, and the brainstorming process ensures that everyone is given an opportunity to contribute to the final outcome. Domineering leadership that stifles debate and creativity is a hindrance to effective revenue risk control.

During a brainstorming session on communications risk, whether for fraud, revenue leakage, cyber security or other issues, the following sequence is may be adopted:

1. *Overview and objective setting*: The coordinator describes the purpose of the session, the products and services under review and provides any other background information such as benchmarking from other companies, known risks and cases, etc.

2. *New service or product mapping*: The shape of the product and service is mapped, possibly on a whiteboard, either as a technical process flow diagram or as a revenue management chain diagram. In many cases, both forms of mapping are needed. A presentation from an expert on the product and service is often useful at this stage.

3. *Open brainstorming session on risks*: The whole group is encouraged to think up all conceivable risks and to relate them to specific areas of the product or service maps (see Figure 3.1 on the following page). The golden rule here is that every idea is accepted and the person leading the session ensures that debate does not occur at this stage. This is a 'brain dumping' activity and there is no such thing as a foolish opinion. The key to a successful brainstorming session is to prevent one or two individual voices from blocking the capture of ideas.

4. *Open discussion*: Each of the risks listed is now discussed in detail. The three primary points to be debated, and possibly supported by statistics, are:

   a) *Frequency*. How common is the manifestation of the perceived risk in the real world, either in relation to the product or service being assessed, or in similar products and services?

   b) *Impact*. What would the impact of each manifestation of the risk be on the product or service, and on the organisation as a whole? Financial, operational and reputational impacts need to be considered.

   c) *Dependency*. Similar to impact, but broken out as a key factor, the dependency of the organisation on the threatened process is assessed. Often, financial impacts weigh more heavily than other effects in the minds of senior managers. Considering dependency separately allows for impacts that are not easily quantifiable in financial terms to also be taken fully into account.

5.   *Risk scoring*: The group then scores all of the risks listed. In many cases this may be done collectively, but in situations where the meeting facilitator feels that some voices are not being heard, a decision to have everyone write down their own scores, and to then consolidate those anonymously, may be appropriate.

6.   *Write up*: The appointed scribe (this always seems to be me!) then writes up the product or service description, the process and revenue stream maps, the risks identified and accepted by the group and the final risk scores for circulation to all involved.

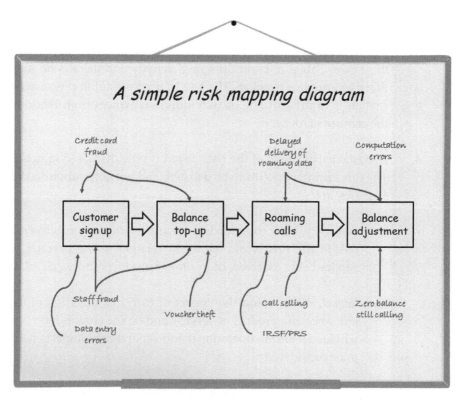

Figure 3.1   Risk mapping diagram

The Importance of Training

Investments in technology are wasted without corresponding investments in the people who will use the technology. Training is generally the most important investment you can make as a skilled team can manage many types of risk using only brainstorming and Excel, but an inadequately trained team won't achieve a thing, even if given the best detection and management systems in the world.

THREE LAWS OF COMMUNICATIONS RISK MANAGEMENT

1. People get promoted until they reach their level of incompetence (the Peter Principle)

2. If something can go wrong it will go wrong (Murphy's Law)

3. When things do go wrong the person responsible for managing the problem will probably be incompetent (Johnson's Law)

The three laws cited above provide the best explanation I can find for the fact that revenue risk teams have been correcting the issues described in the preceding chapters for over 20 years and yet they have still not done themselves out of a job!

The only way to address competence and awareness issues is through in-depth, regular training and awareness activities.

Our approach to training models is to work in line with Bloom's taxonomy (Figure 3.2), a system of classification of learning objectives into six distinct levels for student performance evaluation. The taxonomy is hierarchical; each level is subsumed by the higher levels, so a student functioning at the 'analysis' level has also mastered the material at the 'knowledge', 'comprehension' and 'application' levels. It also provides the basis for the corresponding hierarchy of training methods, as shown on the right in the above diagram.

Developed by psychologist Benjamin Bloom, the taxonomy is considered to be the foundation of learning by many educators. The various levels shown are described here, starting at the bottom.

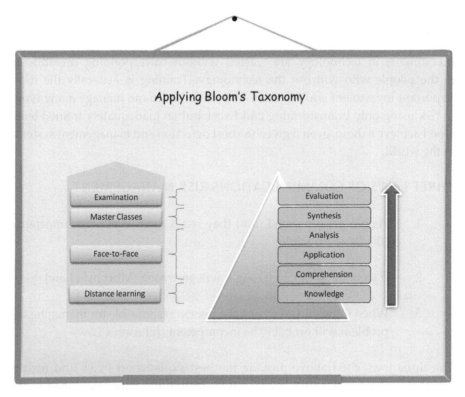

Figure 3.2   Applying Bloom's taxonomy

- *Knowledge level*: Memorising of previously-learned materials by recalling facts, terms, basic concepts and answers (e.g. listing the main types of leakage, fraud or cyber crime).

- *Comprehension level*: Demonstrating an understanding of facts and ideas by organising, comparing, paraphrasing and summarising (e.g. correctly plotting a list of fraud types against a revenue management chain).

- *Application level*: Using new knowledge to solve problems in new situations. Transfer theories to practical situations (e.g. developing a comprehensive list of potential new leakage issues related to a new product or service).

- *Analysis level*: Examining and breaking into components by identifying motives or causes. Drawing conclusions and finding evidence to support generalisations (e.g. successfully investigating a case, determining root causes, establishing accountability and designing corrective and recovery processes).

- *Synthesis level*: Compiling information together in a different way to form new alternatives or solutions. Requires creativity and originality (e.g. developing the specifications for a new set of software features designed to avoid a particular risk from occurring in the future).

- *Evaluation level*: Presenting and defending opinions by making judgments about information. Requires understanding of values. Normally takes the form of essay assignments outside the classroom setting (e.g. writing a business plan, policy and procedures documents, full system requirements specifications or presentations on risk strategy).

Before organising training, therefore, it is essential to assess the current competence and knowledge of every team member in order to prescribe training levels and methodologies that are appropriate to each individual. Simply herding the whole team into a classroom may not be the most effective way to raise the skill levels of everyone involved.

To be effective, risk management training must meet several criteria. Foremost among these are:

- *Planning*: plan the training to address the needs of the recipients.

- *Preparation*: prepare the training and rehearse to ensure problem free delivery.

- *Understanding of the audience*: meet or enquire about the audience's level of knowledge and skill, previous training received and their desired outcomes.

- *Correct setting of expectations*: ensure that your audience knows what your goals are during the event.

- *Subject matter knowledge*: know your topic.

- *The right environment*: comfort, lighting, fully functional technical equipment, acoustics and the provision of regular breaks with access to toilet facilities and refreshments are all essential.

- *Appropriate teaching aids*: use as many aids (e.g. handouts, samples, whiteboards, laptops and projectors, etc.) as needed, but ensure that they are all appropriate to the task. Avoid unnecessary distractions.

- *Appropriate ice breakers and interactivity*: encourage participation but again, keep it appropriate.[1]

- *Professional and engaging delivery*: practice, take feedback and attend presentation training, even if you don't think you need it.

- *Effective confirmation*: develop techniques for ensuring that the students have understood what you have taught.

- *Safe opportunities for feedback*: foster a learning culture in which students can express their views or ask questions freely. I always try to hang around in the classroom after each session while the students file out because there is invariably one person with a question that they were afraid to ask in front of the group.

- *Effective Q&A*: always ensure that you leave adequate time for questions and answers, even if this means cutting the session short.

A Communications Revenue Risk Framework

The control and management of communications revenue risks shares many principles with other high tech security disciplines. A simple ten-point framework captures the key areas to be considered.

1.   *Revenue risk control governance*: This refers to the awareness, organisation and reporting mechanisms in place for employees at all levels to ensure that there is a proper organisational capacity to identify and respond to revenue risks in a timely and effective

---

1   Recently, one of my students jumped up during a break in a lesson and asked whether he could show the class something on my laptop. He then ran a YouTube video containing racist and sexually explicit content, despite the fact that there were several women present!

fashion. The formation of a senior management Risk Committee is a normal first step in this process.

2.   *Risk assessment and planning*: Rather than responding to revenue risks as they manifest themselves, a mature communications operator will have an up-to-date and accurate risk register, with corresponding counter measures, responses and business continuity plans in place, communicated and rehearsed.

3.   *Structure and responsibilities*: The business will have a clearly defined structure for revenue risk management, with responsibilities and mandate properly documented and communicated. In a crisis, the responsible leaders will know that they have authority to respond, the forms of response available to them, and the communications plan that goes with each set of responses.

4.   *Loss prevention framework*: A loss prevention framework maps controls against identified risks, based on perceived or anticipated impact, to achieve the optimum level of protection within the four constraints of budget, headcount, technical capabilities and time.

5.   *Loss prevention technologies*: The framework also encompasses the identification and adoption of relevant and cost-effective technical solutions that address requirements in each phase of the revenue risk control cycle: prevention, detection, mitigation and investigation. Examples are credit-scoring systems, fraud detection systems, RA systems, social media analytics tools and case management applications.

6.   *Revenue risk management processes*: Carefully designed, fully documented and regularly reviewed operational processes for employees, sub-contractors and partners are an essential part of any effective revenue risk control programme.

7.   *Awareness and reputational harm*: Internal and external communications regarding the nature of each revenue risk and the measures required to mitigate it form a key pillar of a successful programme. In particular, reputation management in the event of a major

incident is greatly enhanced when the organisation is able to point to communications measures adopted prior to the event, as well as to technical counter measures established internally. In the age of Twitter and instantaneous global brand damage a Social Media Incident Response Plan is now regarded as an essential part of this communications programme.

8.   *Leakage detection*: This requires recognition that revenue risk events will still occur, preventative steps notwithstanding, and covers the development of capabilities for rapid detection of incidents, in order to minimise their impact.

9.   *New product and service reviews*: Revenue risk assessments do not stop with reviews of existing services. The assessment methodology must be applied to new products and services as well, preferably when they are still under development.

10.   *Key Performance Indicators*: Reporting against KPIs and the use of auditable metrics to measure the success of each control is necessary in order to be able to convincingly demonstrate the revenue risk control business case. Revenue risk control budgets cannot be based purely on manifest losses; they must be based on a combination of known losses, the estimated savings effected and the potential additional future savings or recoveries.

A Short Introduction to Revenue Risk Management Systems

A Revenue Risk Management System (RRMS) is an automated solution designed to collect network and customer data in order to support the creation of alerts on suspect activity and allow investigations and reporting to occur. Some key components of these systems are shown in Figure 3.3.

Revenue Risk Management Systems are widely used within the Telecoms sector to detect possible fraud or leakage events and to investigate and manage cases. A short summary of the key components of such systems is included here, without giving away the confidential aspects of their inner workings which could facilitate fraud.

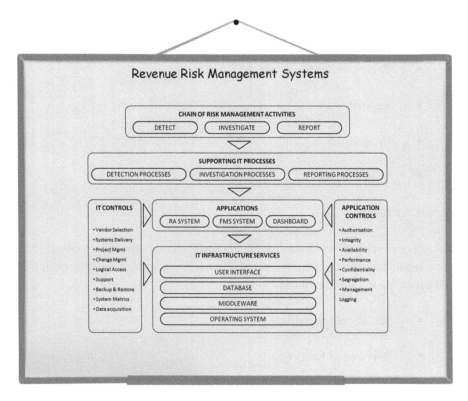

Figure 3.3   Revenue risk system components

THE MAIN LOGICAL COMPONENTS OF AN RRMS

The Dashboard

A Dashboard is designed to communicate key information to users and managers quickly and clearly. A typical dashboard will include multiple charting types and publishing methods such as:

- Publishing: Flash, HTML, Word and more

- Charting: Bar, Pie, Tables, Line, Area, 3D, Speedometer and more

- Key Performance Indicators (KPIs)

The Dashboard will generally focus on reporting of KPIs:

- Alarms or Checks

- Reconciliations

- Reports

- Case statistics

- User activities

Reporting Tools

A number of reports will be available via the system's reporting toolset. These allow technical users and analysts to drill down to a level of detail greater than that provided via the Dashboard:

- Statistical reporting

- Revenue at Risk reports

- Overall Revenue risk reports

- System performance reporting

Alarm Management

Alarm management allows users to view alarms and to filter and sort these by score, value, date, type and similar parameters. The alarm management area is where decisions are made about the validity and relative value of alarms so that the next step, case management, can be undertaken in a structured manner.

Case Management

A case is effectively a folder that holds a set of related alarms and other relevant data. Users work with cases and make decisions about how each case will be handled or concluded. The Case Manager should provide an overview of all open and closed cases.

Decision Support

This may be a part of the Case Manager or a separate component. It allows users to make decisions about each case, forward case details to other teams, compute financial losses and, possibly, to trigger a feedback loop into the rules or other alarm generation engine.

System Configuration and Management

This is where business rules, alarm rules, hot lists user rights and similar matters are managed. The system configuration area can normally only be accessed by a sub-set of trusted users or administrators.

4

Managing Insider Fraud

Contributed by Nick Mann

Introduction

If you ask the question: 'Which of the frauds and crimes that affect my business would be easier to commit from the inside?' the answer, unfortunately, is *all of them*!

Belief and faith in those that work for you is vital and to be encouraged – unquestioning or blinkered trust is not. Knowing your loyal staff and protecting them from the disloyal will reinforce that trust and ensure it is returned.

History and other industry sectors teach us the unpalatable truth that a frightening percentage of our employees, including managers, have the *potential* to go 'bad'. Telephony is a readily marketable commodity in the black marketplace. That, coupled with the fact that we are at the cutting edge of technological advances, means that everything we offer is guaranteed to make the criminal fraternity, inside and outside our business, salivate with greed. In November 2011 CIFAS (The UK Fraud Prevention Service) and the Serious Organised Crime Agency stated that their research had 'indicated that 4.5 per cent of those filed on the CIFAS Staff Fraud Database were assessed as being involved in, or likely to be involved in, serious organised crime'. This figure is probably conservative when applied to the credit service sector, in particular banking and telephony. We will look at further statistics and measurements later in this chapter.

The phenomenal growth rate of the telecommunications industry and its services greatly exceeds the ability, and sometimes the desire, to implement sufficient internal controls. It is unfortunately true to say that until relatively recently most operators concentrated their efforts entirely on external fraud. This was, and to some degree still is, because:

- It is the most obvious problem and time consuming enough on its own

- Nobody likes to think their own people are dishonest

- The relative infancy of the business (particularly mobile telephony) meant we had not experienced the full impact of the internal threat

Attitudes are changing as we learn painful lessons. However, the issue is still one that needs to be nearer to the top of our defence agenda.

Any and all forms of attack have increased effectiveness if they are perpetrated by, or carried out with the collusion of staff. In this chapter we will examine and recommend approaches to prevent, detect and deter this serious business risk.

Note, there is a wide range of departmental structures within which the disciplines of fraud and investigations sit. The merits, or otherwise, of which functions sit with whom are not as important as the existence of a properly trained, resourced and equipped fraud and investigative function that has within its responsibilities all types of internal attack. For simplicity I will refer to the Fraud and Investigations Function (FIF) throughout this chapter.

Types of Attack

There are myriad telephony fraud techniques that can be perpetrated against an operator target and these are dealt with in detail in other chapters. Few of these techniques are specific to insider attacks but the following list highlights some common areas in which fraud often depends on staff involvement in the form of either collusion or neglect:

- Billing

  - Adjustments

- Sales

    - Application processing/compromise of data
    - Commission agreements with channels

- Fraud by CSRs

    - Payments and credits to customer accounts
    - Billing adjustments
    - Handset upgrades
    - Pre-paid credits

These frauds can become very serious when they are committed on a large scale but, as stated, this normally involves an external element. Others can be much more of a concern where there is significant billing or network compromise. Again the latter is normally directed from outside.

Poor Informations & Communications Technology (ICT) security is certainly a major factor, in particular when theft of data is a problem, but the human aspect of the internal threat rarely features prominently in risk assessments or discussions and our focus as a sector always seems to be on technical solutions when the issue of fraud is as much a people problem as it is a technical one; we have yet to see a case involving theft or manipulation of data perpetrated by a machine. It is weaknesses in machine security or business processes that allow such incidents to be perpetrated, but they are perpetrated by people, most commonly insiders.

Highly proficient technical post holders are probably the most sensitive class of employee. If they become miscreants their capacity to steal or manipulate is potentially boundless and their ability to conceal their deeds for long periods of time exacerbates the danger. The simple reason for this that they are often the only people within the business who understand the technology at a deep level. This means that they have access to the most sensitive classes of data, while at the same time nobody else within the organisation has the skills to monitor their activities.

Telephony, like any business, is also susceptible to a wide range of general business frauds and crimes, including procurement fraud, payroll fraud and false financial reporting. Indeed, these can be much more costly and damaging than core business related crimes suc as airtime frauds, especially in a business where our procurement activities are so intensive and diverse. However, many

Operators have no clearly defined ownership for internal fraud control and, in our experience, most lack the capacity to address it effectively.

This is at odds with many other sectors in the credit service industry and it is even more alarming when one considers that frauds such as false financial reporting have been responsible for some very high profile business failures over recent years. Later in the chapter we will examine ways in which operators can protect themselves against the internal threat in any form, drawing lessons from approaches taken in other sectors.

Threat Assessment and Measurement

The starting point for improving the resilience of your organisation to internal attack is to establish where high threat potential exist. It is essential to conduct a comprehensive Internal Threat Review encapsulating the level of exposure and management of all fraud and security issues across the business. Internal Threat Assessment and Measurement (ITAM) is a form of analytical measurement approach designed to clearly determine where high risk (Threat Quotient) employee roles exist within a business, thus enabling the implementation of appropriately targeted, proportional and cost-effective controls.

ITAM exercises identify threat types by role and measure their severity in detail by examining all elements of *opportunity*, *ease/probability* and *impact*. All role types (and role type families) across the organisation are identified with the assistance of the HR team. Volunteers are taken from each role type (or family) and they are then interviewed by experienced threat management professionals. It should be clearly explained to each interviewee that the interview is an objective examination of the threat potential of their *role* and is not about them personally.

Once the interviewer has established exactly how the role is performed, how it relates to other roles and parts of the business, and the controls to which it is subject, the interviewee is invited to explore with the interviewer how an insider with malicious intent could pose a threat to the business.

It is more effective if two interviewers, working separately, conduct the review and the interview product, along with any supplementary information acquired, is jointly examined in detail. This is to ensure that the correct *principle threat* is identified for every role, and that the scoring is uniform. The roles are scored during this examination using the following methodology:

Internal Threat Quotient Scoring Mechanism

Role Opportunity

a)   Level of Authority

b)   Ability to Supervise

c)   Level of Supervision Imposed

d)   Access to Business Element (e.g. Systems, Network, Client Monies and so on)

e)   Ability to Change, Divert or Manipulate that Element

Threat Reality

a)   Ease of Attack

b)   Detection Likelihood

Threat Impact

a)   Financial Effect

b)   Business Element Impact

c)   Damage Limitation/Recovery Possibility

d)   Client/Investor Confidence

e)   Market Reputation

Once the *principle threat* for that role has been determined[1] the 12 criteria listed are scored individually and a calculation algorithm is applied to determine the Threat Quotient. A sample matrix of Roles, Threats and Quotients can be found later in this chapter.

---

1   External threats are included insofar as high internal collusion potential exists.

Table 4.1   A simple ITAM type score sheet

Role	Level of authority	Ability to supervise	Level of supervision imposed	Access to Business Element	Ability to change, divert or manipulate	Total Score		
Threat	Ease of Attack	Detection Possible				**Totals**	÷	**Results**
Threat	Financial Effect	Business Element Impact	Damage Limitation/recovery	Customer/Investor confidence	Market Reputation	**Totals**	X	**Results**
						Total		
						Threat Quotient =		

Once these threat types have been identified and measured, the resilience of the organisation to such events and its ability to manage them is scrutinised. The resulting Threat Quotients highlight the principle threat and threat potential for each role type within the organisation and will determine exactly where and how to apply the controls we will discuss later.

Resource levels will determine where the high threat criticality line is drawn in the Threat Quotient scores but it would be prudent to ensure that at least the top 10 or 15 per cent roles attract most attention in terms of controls in particular pre-employment security screening (vetting).

Although this process may seem arduous it is actually quicker than it appears and will save much greater effort in the medium term, as searching for internal crime can often be like looking for a needle in a haystack. What you now have is a haystack that is a tenth of its former size and you know what needles to look for and in which part of the haystack you are most likely to find them. Total prevention is impossible, but the scope for risk can be diminished considerably through this type of exercise.

Motivations for Internal Attack

In the mid-1940s an eminent criminologist (Donald Cressey) introduced the 'Employee Fraud Triangle', showing the three constituent parts of an employee fraud: rationalisation, opportunity and motivation.

How any individual might rationalise his future actions is naturally difficult to predict with confidence. However, motivation is often quite predictable but is rarely considered before the event. This may represent a missed opportunity to develop logical scenarios that plot the possible course of a range of internal crimes, as well as pulling out the 'markers' that can be monitored in order to detect increased levels of risk. Indeed, a 20-year study (Hollinger and Clark, *Theft by Employees*) based on 12,000 employees concluded that the most common reason employees committed fraud had little to do with opportunity but more with motivation.

TYPES OF MOTIVATION

The KPMG 2007 'Profile of a Fraudster Survey' showed the main fraud motivator to be financial pressure, often arising from excessive lifestyles. No studies have examined the full breadth or depth of motivations for internal crime or their potential relevance in internal fraud/crime management, but an American criminology commentator (Nettler) succinctly summed these up as: 'Babes, Booze and Bets'! Although obviously tongue in cheek, this does cover a large proportion but by no means all. A closer and more exhaustive examination is worthwhile.

There are probably three major classes of motivation (with some crossover):

1. Greed

2. Need

    i.   Debts (self-inflicted)

    ii. Debts (true necessity)

    iii. Targets[2]/survival/concealment of error/deficit

    iv. Coercion/under threat/blackmail

    v.   Addictions: alcohol, drugs, sex, gambling

3. Miscellaneous

    i.   Malice/revenge (existing)

    ii. Malice/revenge (responsive)

    iii. Competitive sabotage

    iv. Peer (or family) pressure/loyalty

    v.   Psychological problems

    vi. Excitement/entertainment/self-aggrandisement/ego

    vii. Idealism/terrorism

---

2   Note that some fraud drivers can actually be imposed by the organisation.

viii. Stupid/naive (i.e. no deliberate motive)

ix.   Mole/cell (i.e. only purpose to employment)

x.   Industrial or state espionage

xi.   Altruism – the 'Robin Hood' syndrome

Many of these motives are well known to us and we frequently witness case examples, but it is worth recording some examples of the less obvious or common to illustrate that all are problematic if ignored:

- Coercion as a driver for fraud has a recent manifestation (June 2010) where a bank cashier helped thieves steal £150,000 after she was threatened with exposure as a bigamist

- In the summer of 2011 a finance director was convicted after stealing £85,000 by using the company credit card to fuel his sex addiction and pay for brothel visits and live internet sex shows, falling into addictions category

- The idealism driver was exemplified by a case in 2006 where alleged terrorists were tape recorded discussing 'targeting utility companies by using recruits with inside knowledge to cut off electricity, water and gas power supplies across the country'

- Peer pressure has a recent example in a mother who spent money stolen from her employers to 'keep up with the Joneses'

- An unusual example of self-inflicted debt is the case in 2009 of the employee who admitted stealing £200,000 from her employers to fund her purchase of 18 show-jumping horses

- Probably the most famous examples of fraud committed to conceal an error are the *Barings* case and the recent case of unauthorised trading by a French Bank trader, both resulting in massive losses for their employers

- In May 2011 a personal assistant at an accountancy firm was convicted of fraud, the court heard that 'she was obsessed with being the centre of attention' and the judge said: 'You used the proceeds to buy friendship and affection' – this would appear to fall into the self- aggrandisement category

- Altruism as a motive for fraud is rare but there was a 2011 case in which an individual gave part of the £370,000 proceeds, defrauded from his employer, to charity

MOTIVATION LINKAGE

It is possible to link most motivations under four main Risk Factor Indicators (RFIs):

Financial

Compulsion

Secret/Embarrassment

Illogical

As we will see, there are opportunities to detect these RFIs in both subjective and objective controls before and after employment.

Making the connection between internal fraud motives and controls has to be done effectively and involves much more than simply devising controls that reflect how attacks are generally perpetrated. Attacks can vary as fraudsters respond to changes in the operating business processes, technology and the controls themselves. Motives, however, are relatively constant and therefore offer better base for devising countermeasures. That said, this is not something that is likely to provide easy wins in the short term but what is certainly evident from above is that it warrants further study.

Controls

Let's take the most difficult and important of these first.

VETTING (PRE-EMPLOYMENT SECURITY SCREENING)

This is the principle tool in the internal threat prevention armoury. Sadly it is rarely applied with sufficient sophistication or even correctly. Even those organisations that do apply vetting controls (beyond asking for references) usually do so in a very unscientific, costly and ineffective fashion where all roles are treated in the same way, or vetting levels are based solely on salary and seniority. Neither of these criteria is particularly relevant in determining what the key risk roles are.

Spotting Risk Factor Indicators requires detailed vetting checks and, realistically, one can only conduct that level of vetting on a small subset of roles. Thus it is necessary to decide which posts carry the highest fraud or corruption risk or criticality. The ITAM process described earlier, whereby we can measure the attack opportunity, ease and impact for each role (or role family) is well suited to this purpose. It enables proportional (the most common legal/regulatory test for 'intrusive' vetting) and targeted vetting controls based on the Threat Quotient scores determined for each role.

Vetting is a huge subject in itself and it is important to understand the legalities within your jurisdiction. A hierarchical system of vetting should be introduced for those roles that represent high internal threat potential and such roles should be subject to enhanced checks (see below). If there are high Threat Quotient roles requiring enhanced checks that have unmanageably high intake numbers (e.g. customer services), random sample candidates should be selected for such enhanced screening. A policy describing this approach is required.

It is paramount that any vetting scheme is conducted within the law and based on three key principles:

- *Voluntary*: all applicants and potential applicants must be made aware of the level of screening from the stage of post advertisement onwards and their consent must be obtained either by inclusion in the Contract of Employment or via a separate document. The subject may decline to offer such data or decline to obtain such data; in this case the future of the recruitment or promotion process in respect of this individual must be carefully considered.

- *Open/Overt*: the subject is entitled to know of the existence and operation of the policy, the data sought and the sources used.

- *Proportionate*: the level and intensity of the screening will be directly proportional to the criticality of the role concerned and must be demonstrably proportionate, i.e. by application of the appropriate Threat Quotient level accorded and/or application of role access levels as described in the Information Classification Treatment control described later.

The type and extent of vetting checks you conduct will be determined by the law in your country. There are some issues that you should be particularly wary about (e.g. ethnicity and sexuality) although in some jurisdictions these points are legitimately included. Some standard checks which should be considered, subject to relevant local legal guidance, are:

- Criminal records checks

- Identity checks

- Credit reference checks

- Electoral roll checks

- Residence checks

- Document verification checks

- Financial sanctions checks

Some enhanced checks that should, if possible and legally acceptable, be included:

- Security interviews with successful candidate at commencement of screening

- Telephone or face-to-face interviews with three candidate referees (chosen from a list of five [three employment and two personal] supplied by the candidate)

- Identity verification of referees

- Financial analysis – the candidate will be asked to supply a statement of all financial outgoings as well as six months' bank and credit/debit card statements (a separate written consent should be obtained including wording that these records will not be copied or retained and returned to the candidate asap), the analysis will attempt to identify any anomalies

- Detailed searches on past and present Directorships held and any disqualifications registered

- Final security interview with the candidate – the candidate must be given an opportunity to answer any anomalies found

Any change of role to a higher level of Threat Quotient criticality should entail re-vetting appropriate for the new role. Regular repeat vetting should also be applied to all high Threat Quotient roles and this should be included in the employment contract or covered by a separate document. An Exit Process (immediate removal of passwords, access control, equipment etc.) for all leavers should also be part of this staff integrity process and the Fraud and Security team must be informed immediately if the leaver's role is of a high/enhanced Threat Quotient level.

Enhanced level reports should contain only information strictly relevant to the screening process. They should be classified as Confidential and held in secure storage. Such reports should be destroyed as soon as they are no longer required. The content of these reports should be discussed with HR in order for them to form a view with line management on the desirability of employment. There is no such thing as a failed screening: it is simply a means of discovering any potential security risk so that it may be managed.

In order to detect the Risk Factor Indicators we discussed earlier, it is important to ensure the following points are covered in a vetting exercise:

- Is the application real?

- Are the applicant's qualifications (if true) consistent with their career path to date?

- If a risk factor is detected, is what the subject does, or has done:
  - A secret (e.g. criminal record, a habit or extra-marital affair)?
  - Expensive to them?
  - A risk because of how often or how much they do it?

- — Embarrassing if revealed/discovered?
- — A risk to them or anyone else?

It is not only possible to screen for motive presence but also feasible to discover any propensity or capability for fraudulent/criminal activity. *The key is to look for the unusual or the inexplicable.* The analysis for RFIs must take into account all subjective as well as objective factors. For example, too much money can be as much an RFI as too little and one man's gambling addiction is another's hobby:

- A £100 a week gambling habit may well pose a risk for a clerk who is only to earn £20k per annum (possible addiction).

- Such a habit is not a risk for a Director who is to earn £100k per annum, probably more of a hobby.

- But, what if he has kept it a secret from his wife? In this case, it becomes a risk regardless of affordability – any keeping of significant secrets that can be found through a vetting process exposes the candidate to coercion in the form of blackmail.[3]

A CASE STUDY

A candidate supplied a CV, references, bank and financial outgoing statements. Examination of the documents and the candidate revealed RFIs of a predisposition to fraud/crime, namely a drugs habit (uncovered by spotting inexplicable cash withdrawals every second Thursday) and forged references (identified because they contained the same misspellings as those spotted in the CV) to cover a dismissal for alleged bribery. This application for employment was rejected.

It is not feasible to spot some motivations prior to employment, often because this is a first time offence and the employment is itself causal to the Motivation and presents the Opportunity (and possibly the Rationalisation). Almost all motivations would become 'vettable' if we applied repeat vetting (on High Risk posts). Repeat vetting would be particularly successful if linked with Fraud Monitoring/Detection and other objective post-employment controls.

---

3   Note, such detailed (Gold Standard) Screenings must be conducted by experienced investigators. This is particularly important in the interviews and analysis of data, e.g. bank accounts.

As we will see later, the UK has seen a 70 per cent increase in unsuccessful employment application frauds, proving, if proof were needed, that serious attempts at screening will produce very beneficial results and that vetting is without doubt the primary internal crime prevention tool.

Whether the motivation or RFI is 'vettable' or not, all motivations and the resultant attack, are susceptible to being controlled. Moreover, it should now be obvious that each control is better applied with knowledge of the range of motivations and their RFIs.

Some of the most important non-technical controls that should be considered are as follows.

EDUCATION AND TRAINING – SECURITY AWARENESS PROGRAMMES

The dangers and impact of fraud and other security breaches must be spelled out to every employee, particularly in those high threat departments highlighted by the Threat Quotients. This is essential for some attacks, such as social engineering, information loss and hacking or computer viruses, and it is advisable that staff are at least made aware of most of the other attack types. Such awareness has several other benefits; it makes honest staff more knowledgeable in terms of what to look for and puts potentially dishonest staff on notice that there is somebody looking and that their own colleagues are now aware of what they might be up to. Education creates an environment that is unfriendly to fraudsters and thieves.

There are some commentators who caution against educating employees on what illegal opportunities are open to them as it might lead to increased criminal activity. However, if the training is delivered by professionals this is not an issue. In any event, those that have or will become fraudsters will not require educating – they will have made it their business to find out what vulnerabilities exist already. What is important here is to be circumspect about what detection mechanisms you have in place as well as the exact modus operandi of the more serious technical attacks, while reinforcing the message that the business is not blind to the risks and has controls in place to prevent or detect losses.

These awareness sessions are an opportunity to 'sell' new policies, to encourage reports to the FIF function and to dispel the myth that this is in some way a betrayal of their colleagues.

Security awareness should not just be a one-off session but a continual programme to raise fraud and security awarenesss across the organisation assisted by training, accessibility and 'testing' from induction to exit.

COMMUNICATION AND INTELLIGENCE

Honest employees must have an easy means of reporting any concerns about colleagues, in confidence or anonymously if they prefer. The same should be put in place for suppliers and contractors. The FIF and HR should operate this jointly and ensure that sufficient controls are in place to prevent malicious or spurious allegations being made (see 'Duty to Report' later in this chapter).

Analytical tools and skills should be utilised to ensure that the complete intelligence analysis cycle is used to process each report received:

- Collection

- Collation

- Evaluation (including Source and Content scoring)

- Analysis

- Dissemination

What in isolation may be simply an odd instance can become a positive suspicion if the correct intelligence protocols are in place.

FOSTERING GOOD INDUSTRIAL RELATIONS

Many of the motivations we looked at earlier originate when staff morale is low and/or industrial relations break down. Not only does dishonesty tend to increase but the likelihood of honest staff reporting their concerns decreases. Thus it is the job of HR to ensure, along with line management, that difficult times are met with good treatment for staff and good times are enjoyed as well. Loyalty from the business, honesty and transparency are usually what staff want most.

REALISTIC TARGET PROGRAMMES

Some of the world's largest and most damaging frauds have resulted from pressure to achieve unrealistic company goals. It is the job of the management chain, the audit function and committee, as well as the non-executive directors to be vigilant, particularly in times of economic downturn.

Reporting and Detection

We have examined the RFIs that may exist in the subjective sense related to an individual's motivation. Such indicators do, of course, also exist in the data we hold, produce or process, although how we can best assess this data for telephony related fraud risks is examined elsewhere in this book.

Unless internal controls are very mature, a large proportion of internal attacks are detected by reports from other employees.

> *There are numerous well-known motivations for staff fraud, from greed, financial hardship through to dissatisfaction or feeling under undue pressure. What this means, therefore, is that an organisation's anti-fraud processes are essential and must never be sacrificed, but the most important aspect for any organisation is its staff. While most are trustworthy, hard-working and honest – an organisation's staff are the first barrier to any bad apples lying inside the workforce, and that an unengaged workforce will provide no barrier to any criminality that might take place.*
>
> *Arjun Medhi, Staff Fraud Adviser,*
> *CIFAS The UK's Fraud Prevention Service*

As such, this critical source of information must be protected, nurtured and developed. There are a couple of simple actions that will dramatically enhance this invaluable intelligence/evidence source.

ONE – DUTY TO REPORT POLICY AND PROCESS

This Policy should make it *mandatory* for all staff to report suspicions of dishonesty, malpractice or security compromise to the FIF. This is separate to any whistle-blowing process but can be made part of it. Thus whistle-blowing becomes mandatory, not merely voluntary, and the employee is encouraged to make the report to the FIF (anonymously if they wish). The 'Duty to Report' should be included in induction training along with fraud and security awareness and all staff and newcomers should be made to sign it as part of their Contract of Employment.

TWO – INVESTIGATIVE ENGAGEMENT POLICY AND PROCESS

The lines between evidence collection and disciplinary action are often confused within organisations. Thus only appointed and trained investigations staff (i.e. FIF) should conduct internal investigations. There should be no line management or HR participation or interference in evidence collection or interview process. This is to ensure the integrity and independence of evidence collection and to remove any possibility of conflicts of interest. Moreover, it engenders trust in the staff that their concerns will be handled by professionals. Similarly, investigators should not be directly involved in the disciplinary process (including disciplinary or exit interviews) or decision on punitive action, although investigators should participate by formulating opinions on the likely success of prosecution or the necessity for police involvement. It is imperative that the FIF investigators are given this investigative mandate which should be endorsed by the Chief Executive/President/Chairman.

> Note, the Internal Audit function is sometimes given the role of investigator in 'normal business fraud'. This is not ideal and can be a source of confusion where a Fraud and Investigation function exists. Whoever is given the responsibility, the meaning of the term 'investigation' should be clearly defined, i.e. does it refer to the collection of admissible evidence, and has the requisite training been given or expertise recruited?

Often staff state during reviews that they would have reported previous internal incidents had the above policies and facilitation been in place. Moreover, where such policies have been introduced there has been a significant rise in the number and quality of such reports.

Specific 'Normal Business Frauds'

Whole books have been dedicated to this subject and as stated earlier, this chapter is intended to deal with the internal threat. That said, telephony readers may benefit from some basic comments on the controls required to address two leading 'normal business frauds'.

PROCUREMENT FRAUD

All procurement should be centralised and must include a fully authorised and recorded purchase order system including a tendering process. The FIF team should conduct due diligence on all new large or 'critical' suppliers and spot checks on all elements of the purchasing lifecycle. Policy (and related processes) should provide tight but practical controls to ensure adherence, e.g. a sensible de minimis[4] for individual department purchase. Departments should be responsible for sign-off of delivery against order, reportable to central procurement. The policy and process must include separation of roles/ responsibility against order/new supplier, delivery confirmation and payment. An auditable Gift Register should also be kept by all departments. Decisions on de minimis levels for register entry should be sensible but deliberate failure to make a prescribed entry should be deemed a matter of 'Dishonest Gross Misconduct'.

FINANCIAL REPORTING FRAUD

This is an issue which has its motivation and opportunity within senior management and the finance department. The drive behind Sarbanes-Oxley requirements over the past decade (for businesses whose shares are listed or traded in any way in the USA) has its roots in this crime, i.e. the Enron and WorldCom scandals.

The common mistake here is that financial controls, visibility and 'fraud detection' are usually left within the remit of the finance department itself. In some mature businesses the Internal Audit function (with oversight by an Audit Committee) has some independent responsibility and power in this respect, although even there the FIF team rarely plays an active role.

This is not an area easily policed by non-financial experts. The solution lies in developing close operational co-operation between the Internal Audit and FIF teams with the latter being given greater training and being encouraged to recruit expertise in this field. The greater use of new monitoring and detection engines should also improve capabilities and facilitate the earlier discovery of malpractice.

Implementation of the Investigative Engagement and Duty to Report Policies referred to earlier, will ensure autonomy and investigative power as well as facilitation for finance and senior management to report concerns.

---

4   Minimal levels considered 'trifling' – a level of risk too small to be concerned with.

FIF Reporting Lines

Because of the possibility of investigation of Senior Management and the Executive/Board itself, as well as other key directorates such as the Finance department, it is important to give some thought to the reporting lines of the Fraud and Investigation Function (FIF). The key objectives are autonomy and empowerment.

As such it is important for the FIF to have a non-functional (i.e. not one of the key business functions such as finance, technology, customer services) reporting line for the following reasons:

- Many aspects of its work are, of necessity, conducted across all of the business silos. If FIF is owned by any functional directorate its independence will be compromised.

- To enable objectivity of engagement across all units of the business and to be listened to, respected and trusted, FIF must be seen to have no alternative interest or agenda other than its own objectives.

- Internal security and investigations can be centered on *any* function at *any* rank – investigating one's manager or colleague is neither practical nor desirable. This is more likely in a functional directorate such as finance, technology and customer services, as these are where the most opportunities for internal compromise exist.

- Some functional directorates may be more problematic than others in terms of achieving their objectives with applicable and relevant KPIs:

  - Finance:

    ○ Less understanding of the unquantifiable value of deterrent and prevention and reliance on fraud figures/ percentage when low figures can mean either excellent Fraud Management or, as likely, failure to detect
    ○ Lack of understanding of non-financial threats, impacts or losses
    ○ Financial Reporting Fraud conflict

- Technical:

  ○ Over reliance on technical solutions and defences
  ○ Lack of understanding of non-technical attacks

There is a necessity for FIF to be independent of these directorates. Options for FIF reporting include direct reports to CEO/President/Chairman, Legal and Regulatory Director, the Company Secretary, a Non-Executive Director or the Audit Committee.

It is also key to the success of any FIF, that their direct report should be someone who personally has empathy for the work in which they are engaged and the gravitas to support FIF at senior levels.

Response, Investigations and Deterrent

The objectives of any investigation should be to:

- Provide a deterrent

- Collect admissible evidence and ensure the integrity of same

- To recover any lost assets, monies

- Inhibit or stem any further losses

- Minimise disruption to business

- Defend business reputation and retain customer and investor confidence

- Prevent/reduce harmful effect on staff morale

- Enact immediate operational damage limitation

If the investigative process is conducted by experienced professionals, most of the above will be achievable. They will also ensure that evidence is collected in accordance with best practice in that jurisdiction, and that all punitive options are retained. It is often the case that what starts as a relatively small enquiry that you may wish to deal with by way of a disciplinary caution evolves into a highly complex case involving substantial losses/damage. If the evidence has not been correctly collected from the beginning, the option of prosecution that you will now probably wish to use, may well have been lost as the evidence has become inadmissible. Thus it is recommended that managers are prohibited from confronting suspects prior to referral to the FIF (see Investigative Engagement Policy). Other staff will also be more comfortable if the problem is dealt with swiftly and professionally.

If you have experienced in-house investigators who can be utilised it is not advised that the Police are called in until the investigation is reaching its conclusion. *The Police will not have the same set of business objectives as you.* As long as the evidence has been collected and secured properly the Police should be comfortable. In fact they are more likely to accept the case if it does not tie up their resources because the bulk of the work has been done for them in the correct manner by your properly trained staff. You should also consider civil routes to asset recovery, e.g. freezing of suspect employee bank accounts.

The FIF should not determine the punitive route to be followed. That is a matter for HR and/or line Board. If prosecution is the opted for, consideration might be given to seeking PR advice in order to maximise deterrent (inside and outside the business) and minimise confidence/reputation loss.

It is also important to ensure that the modus operandi (MO) of the fraud/crime is examined closely in order to be able to enhance prevention, protection, detection and intelligence mechanisms. This is often described as the 'feedback loop' or 'lessons learned' process. Correspondingly, each time a new case is detected, the motivation together with the modus operandi (MO) and ease of opportunity needs to form part of a reassessment of the ITAM threat analyses described earlier.

It is still rare for cases of serious internal dishonesty to be reported to the authorities. This certainly should be a resort that is used judiciously but nevertheless one which needs to be part of the armoury of deterrence. Often, in countries with immature law enforcement agencies, reports are not made by businesses as the authorities have neither the desire nor the ability to respond, which is all the more reason for the case to be investigated professionally within. However, even in the UK, 73 per cent of CIFAS (UK Fraud Prevention Service) cases are not reported to the Police despite the fraud being proven and confirmed and the CIFAS Member having reasonable grounds to press charges.

If the PR aspects are handled correctly, the prosecution of an organisation's miscreants can become a positive signal to customers and investors, illustrating that is the business is able and willing to deal with its 'bad apples', improve its resilience and thus become a more secure and stable enterprise.

Measurement, Reporting and Sharing

> *It is of great concern that in my experience many organisations in most sectors, including telephony, have no adequate system of recording or measuring the full range of internal crime. Thus there is no true ability to share trends let alone attempt concerted prevention or response. This coupled with the fact that in many organisations no one department, for example Fraud and Security, have the responsibility or mandate to investigate all internal crime, so in many cases the opportunity to identify control weaknesses and share these across the organisation is lost.*
>
> Colin Yates, Head of Group Fraud and Investigations for Vodafone
> and former Deputy Chair and Head of the GSM Association
> Fraud Forum Intelligence Sub-Group

This inability to share best practices and crime trends, let alone intelligence, with the authorities would be considered unacceptable in relation to external fraud cases and should be equally so for internal crime.

Overcoming the reluctance to report is not the only issue. There is often a recording model present in many firms that has a focus principally on external fraud, making an accurate, measurable record of the instance difficult or impossible to construct. This is frequently the case in the credit services sector (including telephony) where the preponderance of frauds, in terms of sums defrauded and numbers of cases, is external. Another common error is to misreport incidents by referring to the core fraud type (e.g. 'financial fraud') without reference to the internal element. A dedicated unit/person within the organisation, who is responsible for internal fraud management and who can act as a single point of contact, will ensure that these issues are overcome.

It is difficult to effect wholesale change like this for an industry, but the various Fraud Associations can play an important part and appoint officers whose primary role is to address the area of internal fraud, in particular measurement and reporting, the provision of appropriate training offerings and the development of user-friendly standard recording models. Certainly, where we have seen this being done, the accuracy and utility of internal fraud reports dramatically increases.

Statistics

Available internal fraud measurements and statistics are normally based on surveys, are often limited, or are based on the few cases that reach the prosecution stage. It is also the case that many countries produce no statistics at all on employee fraud/crime. This may be due to a cultural block or simply because they do not have the means for effective measurement and reporting. A global perspective on internal fraud losses is not really currently achievable as a result. Uniquely, the UK through its Fraud Prevention Service, has developed a Staff Fraud Database which it launched in 2006. Limited as the figures are, they do still provide some useful pointers. Here is a selection of recent observations:

- KPMG Fraud Barometer (which measures fraud based on cases of £100,000+ losses and reported to Crown Court): Internal fraud committed by employees (of all levels of seniority) also did £225m worth of damage this year (up from £181 million January–June 2010), with management fraud, averaging at £7.3 million a case, and employee fraud around £708,000.

- The accountancy firm BDO Stoy Hayward collates data from all reported fraud cases over £50,000 (reported to the Courts and Media). For 2011 they reported employee fraud was down to 10 per cent (of all reported fraud) from 14 per cent last year. However, they also reported that cases of corruption were steadily increasing from less than 1 per cent in 2009 to just under 2 per cent in 2010 to 4 per cent in 2011.

- Kroll Consulting in its 2010/11 Global Fraud Report (commissioned by them and carried out by the Economist Intelligence Unit who surveyed 800 Senior Executives globally) showed that for those companies affected by fraud, 22 per cent of instances were perpetrated by junior employees 22 per cent by senior ones and 11 per cent by agents or intermediaries. Thus 'the proportion of fraud carried out by those who work for the company in one way or another goes way above half'. Moreover the report stated: 'The finding is remarkably consistent across geographies'.

In the first six months of 2011, CIFAS (the UK Fraud Prevention Service) Members reported a 24 per cent increase in 'Dishonest action by staff to obtain a benefit by theft or deception'. Some other useful figures from their Staff Fraud Database:

- Even after taking into account the small 3 per cent decrease in 2010, staff fraud has still increased by over 40 per cent since 2008.

- A 63 per cent increase in instances of staff unlawfully obtaining or disclosing personal data was recorded in 2010, with younger age groups more likely to be involved.

- More established members of staff are committing frauds. The average length of time in employment before the fraud was discovered increased to 5.5 years from 4.3 years in 2009.

- The economic uncertainty of recent years, combined with an ever more competitive job market, has led to more and more people attempting to gain employment fraudulently; the 70 per cent increase in unsuccessful employment application frauds indicates that organisations are increasingly checking applications for fraud before recruitment procedures are completed.

The Future as it Relates to Internal Fraud Control

Unquestionably, the development of internal fraud detection engines will have a dramatic impact on the early detection ability but we must have the resources, expertise, ability and the desire to respond and to exploit these solutions. Too often, we see sophisticated software and IT platforms lying unused and forgotten in the depths of operator's technical facilities.

Hopefully, this developmental trend, along with more in-depth research into the topic, will drive some of the vital changes in approach that we have described as necessary to give this category of risk the attention it deserves.

Parts of this chapter (mainly those dealing with Motivations) first appeared in a paper by Nick Mann, 'Examining Motivations for Internal Attack' published as part of 'The Internal Betrayal', a special report by CIFAS (The UK's Fraud Prevention Service) released in August 2010.

About the Contributor: Nick Mann

Nick is an internationally recognised Threat Management and Fraud and Security innovator with over 30 years' experience across the complete spectrum of corporate security and fraud disciplines.

Having begun his career with the Inland Revenue, he moved on to British Telecom, the London Stock Exchange, and IMRO before building the Security and Investigation Department at Orange plc. He has been a director of two international risk management consultancies specialising in telecoms and financial services; Praesidium and Stork Ltd. For five years, until May 2009, Nick was the Director of Fraud, Risk and Security for the Vodafone Group (Global). During this time he was also Chairman of the GSMA (Global Mobile Industry) Fraud Forum for two and a half years.

He now runs his own Fraud and Security consultancy specialising in Strategic Risk and Internal Threat Management: www.nickmannassociates.com

5

Money Laundering and Corruption

An Overview of E-Money

Electronic money (e-money) is now a well-established means of exchange; credit card balances and payments are one form of e-money. However, the emergence of new forms, some of which are unregulated and thus fall outside the formal sector, means that a fresh wave of interest in this type of payment mechanism has arisen. Mobile money and e-payments are of special relevance to telecom operators as they introduce varieties of mobile payment technologies in selected markets. In the UK, Barclays Bank has launched its own mobile payments service, independently of the operators.

The UK's Financial Services Authority defines e-money as monetary value, as represented by a claim on the issuer, which is:

- Stored on an electronic device

- Issued on receipt of funds

- Accepted as a means of payment by persons other than the issuer

However, as I will explain later in the chapter, unregulated e-money services have also emerged. Some of these seem to have appeared almost by accident, while others are clearly designed to circumvent the established systems of control and monitoring and to reduce the cost of financial transactions.

AML, CFT and Tax Evasion Considerations

While mobile money challenges are relatively new, there are existing models in the financial services sector that illustrate when and to what extent a communications operator must start to comply with Anti-money Laundering (AML) and Countering Funding for Terrorism (CFT) regulations and best practice guidelines. Not surprisingly, the greater an operator's involvement in the delivery of financial services (the evolutionary path shown below is typical), the greater the burden of AML and CFT regulation will become.

WHAT IS MONEY LAUNDERING?

As potentially innocent participants in money laundering cases, regulated firms stand to have their reputations tarnished when money laundering cases are proven, and they may also be judged to be non-compliant with regulations governing the sector, resulting in punitive action.

Money laundering refers to any action deliberately taken to conceal the proceeds of crime. It differs from tax evasion in the sense that the money is considered tainted at the outset, and the goal of those engaged in money laundering is to process these funds so as to make them appear legitimate. Money laundering cases typically involve a number of transactions between businesses set up for the purpose and via banking houses that are generally unaware of what is being done.

Classic money laundering is a three-step process, although it is important to recognise that each case will be unique and some steps may be omitted or radically altered:

1. *Placement*: The illicit funds are introduced into the financial system, for example through a fake retail operation that accepts cash payments but which delivers no goods of value.

2. *Layering*: This involves a series of complex financial transactions, commonly by way of numerous accounts in several different institutions and countries. This is done to conceal the source of funds and confuse investigators.

3. *Integration*: This is the final step whereby the laundered funds are passed to the final beneficiary.

RESPONSIBILITY FOR ANTI-MONEY LAUNDERING CONTROLS

In order to comply with the Bank Secrecy Act (BSA), the Third EU Money Laundering Directive and other international AML regulations and guidelines, financial institutions are required to implement anti-money laundering controls internally. These include Customer Due Diligence ('CDD') controls, applied when new accounts are being opened, as well as 'Know Your Customer' or 'KYC' arrangements and Suspicious Transaction Reporting ('STR') mechanisms for existing accounts.

As Figure 5.1 illustrates, communications firms are now moving into financial services terrain and many need to become more active in the AML/CTF arena and better informed about their likely responsibilities. This is not merely a matter of appointing a Money Laundering Reporting Officer (MLRO) and then moving on. There is an entire business process, often supported by technology to raise automatic red flag alerts in high transaction volume environments.

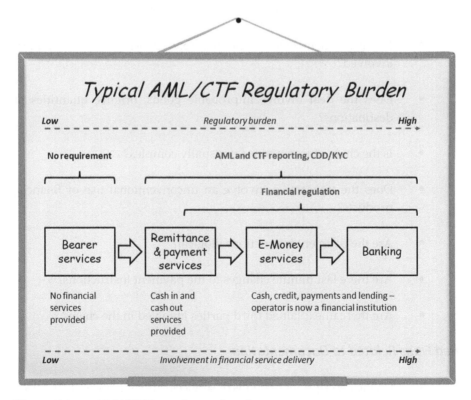

Figure 5.1   AML/CTF regulatory burden

UNDERSTANDING THE AML RED FLAG SYSTEM

An important element of the anti-money laundering regime is gathering financial intelligence through suspicious activity reports. Dr Liliya Gelemerova of Nardello and Co. notes that there is a range of 'red flags' or indicators that can be used by the financial services sector to identify suspicious financial activity. Such financial activity can include managing and laundering the proceeds of crime, terrorist financing and fraud. She further notes that 'red flags' vary depending on the nature of the business, the type of product and type of transaction. Some indicators are geared more specifically towards identifying risks arising from cash-based underground economies such as human trafficking and illegal drugs trade. The list of indicators below can be applied in the area of trade finance but can be recommended to be used also in other financial services areas. It is not an exhaustive list and may not be entirely relevant to the bulk of communications sector transactions today, but it provides a good basis for the development of an appropriate model for assessing transactions.

Red Flags Relating to the Structure of a Transaction

- Is the payment beyond the apparent capacity of the customers involved?

- Does the deal involve improbable goods, origins, quantities or destinations?

- Is the chain of transactions unusually complex?

- Does the transaction involve an unconventional use of financial products?

- Are the payment instructions illogical?

- Are there last minute changes to the payment instructions?

- Are there unexplained third parties involved in the chain?

Red Flags Related to Documentation

- Do the descriptions of goods or services differ significantly between various documents?

- Are shipping documents missing?

- Are copies of documents supplied when originals are required?

- Are mandatory parts of the documents missing?

- Are there blatant misrepresentations concerning the values or quantities of goods or services?

- Are the goods to be supplied 'dual use' and if so, have been accurately described as such in the documents?

Red Flags Relating to the Countries/Parties Involved

- Are any of the countries/parties listed for sanctions or on terrorist lists, or have they been defined by the FATF as having AML deficiencies?

- Are any of the parties named on a watch list, including PEP indices?

- Does the remittance profile match the business profile?

- Are there signs of the disguised involvement of particular countries in the deal?

THE MAIN REQUIREMENTS FOR EFFECTIVE AML

A number of leading international financial institutions have come together to form the Wolfsberg Group, which focuses on defining and promulgating effective anti-money laundering guidelines that complement the existing regulatory framework. These are behind a transition by most jurisdictions to a risk-based AML approach which calls for segmentation of suspected cases based on country risk, customer risk, services risk and transaction risk, to arrive at an overall risk score per event.

Some of the key components of an effective anti-money laundering programme, as recommended by my firm, are:

- Training of staffers

- Risk scoring of customer details

- Profiling and trending analysis routines to detect behavioural deviations

- Automated alerting and case management mechanisms

- Suspicious transaction/activity reporting procedures

- Data retention and audit capabilities to support post-event investigations

- Case management and investigation capabilities designed to identify perpetrators

Depending on the level of risk, Liliya Gelemerova recommends some further Enhanced Due Diligence procedures with regards to customers, agents, subcontractors and third parties:

Public Record Searches

- Media and internet searches, including blogs and social media sites

- Corporate records and other relevant business information searches (e.g. bankruptcy/insolvency records and litigation records)

- Regulatory filings

- Records on public procurement tenders

- Sanctions and watch lists

Discreet Enquiries (Normally Outsourced)

- Red flag verification

- To fill gaps in public records

- To balance potentially biased media reporting

DESCRIPTION OF THE MOST IMPORTANT MANDATED OBLIGATIONS

The main AML obligations to be met by regulated firms are:

1. *Systems and staff training*: to prevent money laundering, covering the training of employees and the establishment of procedures of internal control and communication.

2. *Identification procedures*: to provide evidence of the identity of customers. This must be adapted, particularly for those situations when customers are not physically present.

3. *Record-keeping procedures*: which include keeping copies of identification data for a defined period. This in turn introduces additional data protection requirements, with implications for both ICT and physical security.

Financial institutions should also undertake CDD measures in following situations:

*   When establishing a business relationship

*   When carrying out occasional transactions

*   When there is a suspicion of money laundering or terrorist financing

*   When there are doubts raised about previously obtained customer identification data

Throughout the business relationship regulated firms are required to conduct ongoing due diligence of the relationship and to monitor all transactions undertaken by the customer. The regulated firms have to ensure that the transactions being conducted are consistent with the institution's knowledge of the customer, their business and risk profile, including where necessary validation of the customer's sources of funds.

DEMONSTRATING DUE DILIGENCE

Every financial institution is required to have its own money laundering reporting officer (MLRO) who is responsible for ensuring that the firm establishes and maintains effective systems and controls for compliance with the various requirements and standards under regulatory systems, and for countering the risk that the firm might be used for financial crime. The MLRO sets compliance policies and delegates responsibilities for effective risk rating and monitoring of individuals and transactions to operational teams. The emphasis is thus on the experience, training and skills of the operational teams and the effectiveness of the firm's internal processes and controls for effective compliance management.

THE BUSINESS REPERCUSSIONS OF FAILING TO PREVENT MONEY LAUNDERING

Failure to establish suitable and effective controls, processes and policies would have serious and damaging repercussions to a financial firm. It is an offence, potentially leading to prison terms and/or fines for responsible staffers, for firms to fail to comply with Money Laundering Regulations. Serious breaches are also widely publicised by the regulator and can have far-reaching and long-term effects on an organisation's brand and reputation.

Countering Terrorist Funding

Terrorist funding is conceptually very similar to money laundering, in that the sources and final destinations of funds may be concealed, but it has some very important differences that make it much harder to detect:

1. The movement of terrorist funds generally precedes the commission of the terrorist act, whereas money laundering generally occurs following the commission of a crime.

2. The sums required to fund a terrorist cell are typically only a small fraction of those moved in most money laundering cases. For example, the 9/11 Commission in the United States concluded that the total cost of organising the series of attacks carried out on September 11, 2001, was not more than $500,000.[1] Money laundering cases, on the other hand, regularly involve sums running into many millions of dollars.

---

1   See www.9-11commission.gov/report/911Report_Exec.htm

Watching out for terrorist financing does not necessarily mean watching out for 'tainted' money. Terrorism can be funded with money of legitimate origin. Consequently, except in instances where CDD procedures have triggered alarms, monitoring of terrorist funding is either intelligence led or post-event; 'right of bang' in military parlance. Therefore, the secure retention of both customer and transactional data is crucial in such cases and this represents the main mechanism for ensuring compliance and demonstrating due diligence.

Beneficial Ownership and PEPs

When it comes to due diligence in an international context, there is no one size fits all approach, and each firm must make its own decisions about what constitutes a meaningful response. Some states prefer rules-based models as a means for ensuring that everyone within the jurisdiction applies the same standards of care, although these may lack flexibility.

The core requirements of the evolving KYC/CDD model for tax evasion, AML and CFT recommend by The Wolfsberg Group, and others, are outlined here.

1.   *Establishing Beneficial Ownership*: this refers to a requirement to verify the ultimate owner of a business (not necessarily the registered owner) and the percentage stakes held.

2.   *Validation of Identity*: the process of validating that the named directors actually exist.

3.   *Identifying Politically Exposed Persons (PEPs)*: establishing which customers are PEPs and then developing a risk-based approach to how they are given financial services packages, based on:

     − Geography
     − Customer profile and risk score
     − Products or services requested
     − The provenance of their funds

DEFINING PEPS

The Wolfsberg Guidelines include an FAQ on PEPs that states:

> *Relationships with PEPs may represent increased risks due to the possibility that individuals holding such positions may misuse their power and influence for personal gain and advantage or for the personal gain or advantage of family and close associates. Such individuals may also use their families or close associates to conceal funds or assets that have been misappropriated as a result of abuse of their official position or resulting from bribery and corruption. In addition, they may also seek to use their power and influence to gain representation and/or access to, or control of legal entities for similar purposes.*

> *It is however important to understand that the majority of PEPs do not abuse their position and will not represent any undue additional risk to a Financial Institution solely by virtue of that categorization.*

Although the concept of PEPs is not defined in detail, it is deemed to extend to close associates or close family members. For the presence of a PEP to affect the status of an organisation (i.e. a prospective or existing corporate client of the operator), the PEP would normally need to be a beneficial owner.

Wolfsberg cites the following as examples of PEPs:

- Heads of state, heads of government and ministers

- Senior judicial officials

- Heads and other high-ranking officers holding senior positions in the armed forces

- Members of ruling Royal Families with governance responsibilities

- Senior executives of state-owned enterprises

- Senior officials of major political parties

KYC AND CDD CHALLENGES AND KEY ISSUES FOR OPERATORS

The impact of data protection and privacy laws has worked against CDD/KYC in many environments, with regulated firms being to some extent damned if they do and damned if they don't. There is a big push for change taking place internationally to allow more information to be exchanged, but the cross-border exchange of data can still be a challenge.

In some cases, for example proliferation finance for weapons of mass destruction (WMD), the law has not yet caught up, although changes are reportedly coming, and while there is a need for more and better intelligence, the principles are the same.

Nevertheless, staff awareness of these complex emerging issues is critical as reputational risk is at stake given the politically charged nature of many of these issues. Some of the other financial services risks that employees need to be trained on include, but are not limited to:

- Cyber crime

- Identity theft

- Social engineering via social media

- Insider dealing and other internal threats

- Corrupt money and the appropriation of state assets

- UK Bribery Act issues

- People trafficking

An AML/CFT 'To-Do List' for Telecom Operators

Here is a to-do list for AML and CFT planners that you can use to guide your deliberations:

1. PEP lists:

    a) Which PEP lists should you apply?

    b) Do you construct your own PEP lists or do you buy in lists from external providers?

    c) Do you build or buy your name-matching engine?

2.   Transaction profiling scope:

    a)   Do you make currency specific distinctions?

    b)   Which transactional message types move value?

    c)   Which level of fuzzy matching is appropriate?

    d)   Is it reasonable to exclude some payment types?

    e)   Do you employ two eyes checking or four eyes checking?

3.   Transaction profiling approach:

    a)   Do you process alerts onshore, offshore or is this outsourced, and how does this affect:

        i.   Security

        ii.   Timeliness of response

        iii.   Time zone challenges

    b)   What record fields have value for screening?

    c)   How will you keep business as usual going while also improving processes?

    d)   What do you tell customers when they trigger a hit?

    e)   Can you enforce the use of unique customer IDs across the global enterprise?

4.   Suspicious transaction analysis:

    a)   How will you differentiate between money laundering, terrorism, proliferation, corruption and e-crime?

    b)   How will you address the challenge of unregulated financial transactions:

      i.   Via mobile data links?

     ii.   Via other ISPs or banking services using your subscriber's handsets?

AML/CFT SANCTIONS REGIME CHALLENGES FOR OPERATORS

In order for it to be effective, your AML/CFT sanction screening programme has to be real time and preventative. If this is not the case, criminals will simply identify the window of opportunity and work within that.

To illustrate the complexity of the challenge, one leading bank told us that it employs the following automated AML/CFT controls:

- Twenty-three detection algorithms

- With each algorithm having seven severity settings

- With each severity setting having seven filtering modes

- Plus eight exclusion classes for various record types

- Plus fuzzy matching on account holder names, beneficiary names, business names and addresses

One of the main issues facing operators who want to procure an automated AML toolset is that the requirements for these systems are still poorly defined and there are many different types of tool on the market. Factory default settings are still used by many banks because the analysis needed to establish what the appropriate settings should be has not been done. In addition, most tools and supporting business processes are not regularly reviewed or updated. Smaller firms are hindered by a lack of awareness, as well as inadequate tooling and process design and limited procurement budgets.

In other words, the AML/CFT initiative in the financial services sector appears to be less advanced and much less effective than most outsiders would probably assume.

The first step for an operator entering the financial services regime is to clearly articulate the key financial crime risk challenges it may face, including:

- AML

- CFT

- PEPs

- Bribery and corruption

- Sanctions regimes

Consistency of review and business processes across group structures is the next important facet of control, as well as the design of imaginative measures to address the requirements of training and to deal with staff boredom and frustration resulting from high numbers of false positive alarms.

KEY STEPS

The key steps that an operator should consider when preparing for AML/CTF risks and the related regulatory burden are listed here:

- *Risk assessment*: establish your exposure both to crime and to punitive penalties.

- *Requirements*: define the requirements of an appropriate AML/CTF programme and agree these internally and then with the relevant regulatory bodies.

- *Technology selection*: review and select your technology platforms for suspicious activity reporting (your Telecom Fraud Management System may be capable of fulfilling this role) and PEP name matching.

- *Optimisation*: devise the most cost-effective approaches to meeting your obligations.

- *Assurance and benchmarking*: include reviews of this area in the audit plan and establish KPIs based on industry benchmarks for Risk Committee reporting.

Implications of the UK Bribery Act, 2011

At the time of writing, the UK Bribery Act was about to come into force after an exhaustive, and possibly exhausting, consultation and review process. This new legislation is expected to consolidate several existing laws and simplifies the investigation and prosecution of bribery and corruption offences. The act, in draft form, appears to have implications for businesses worldwide as it covers the overseas operations of all UK businesses and also because it is likely to influence political and legislative elsewhere. The act reflects a general legislative trend and it enshrines principles that are likely to be mirrored by other pieces of legislation in other jurisdictions over the coming months or years.

IMPACT OF THE ACT

The most significant impact of the Act will be the effect it has on UK incorporated entities and foreign registered organisations that carry out business in the UK, directly or through subsidiaries, whether these activities occur in the UK or elsewhere. The act now carries a specific, criminal offence if a commercial organisation fails to prevent an act of bribery.

RELEVANCE OUTSIDE THE UK

The matter of corporate liability will be of particular relevance to commercial organisations that rely upon overseas agents, introducers or business partners to gain or retain business. The onus of liability for the conduct of these third parties may be placed upon the UK incorporated entity, including the UK arm of a foreign registered business. Findings of guilt in the criminal court could lead to a criminal conviction against the commercial organisation and a fine.

ONLY ONE DEFENCE

The draft act provides only one defence against prosecution for this offence – that the commercial organisation had 'adequate procedures' in place to prevent bribery. If an investigation or prosecution is launched against an organisation, these adequate procedures will be subject to close scrutiny by investigators, prosecutors and the criminal courts to determine whether enough was done to prevent bribery.

BURDEN OF PROOF

The burden of proof in such cases is expected to be on the UK commercial organisation, which must demonstrate that adequate procedures were in place. Offences under this act, as drafted, will be prosecuted by the UK Serious Fraud Office, the Police, the Crown Prosecution Service, and Her Majesty's Revenue and Customs. This means that commercial organisations could face investigation by a range of law enforcement bodies. Therefore it is essential that all commercial organisations have in place robust, comprehensive and adequate procedures to prevent bribery.

UK GOVERNMENT GUIDELINES

The UK government has published draft guidelines to assist commercial organisations in understanding what should be included within the adequate procedures they devise. Key messages are that:

- Commercial organisations may take a flexible, proportionate approach in devising adequate procedures, depending on the resources available to the organisation and the level of risks faced in the business they conduct

- There will be no legal requirement that adequate procedures are devised, and no separate inspection regime imposed on commercial organisations, but larger organisations will be expected to have well-developed procedures and strategies in place

A RISK-BASED APPROACH

The guidelines also suggest a principles and risk-based approach, with the following components:

1.   Risk assessments

2.   Top level commitment

3.   Due diligence

4.   Clear, practical and accessible policies and procedures

5.   Effective implementation

6.   Monitoring and review

6

ICT and Cyber Security Risks in Telecoms

Introduction to ICT and Cyber Security

I am currently working on the second book in this series which will also be published by Gower Publishing, probably in late 2013. While that work will cover ICT and Cyber Security risks in more detail, it would be remiss of me not to address the topic from a Telecom perspective here.

The reader will by now have noted the dependency of Information Communications Technology (ICT) on sound cyber security arrangements. ICT security has become a matter of strategic import in the modern economy. Indeed, the UK government now lists cyber security attacks as one of the top national security risks.

Open the newspaper on any given morning, or browse it online, and you will almost invariably see two or three stories about different cyber security breaches, crimes or incidents. These reports underscore the increasing importance of effective cyber security in our digitally connected world, and show what the impact on organisations and individuals can be when cyber-security measures fail or are bypassed, or when the capabilities of the internet are dishonestly manipulated. Some of our own clients are already introducing corporate cyber security controls that capture and store all online activity by employees, including the content (text, images, video and audio) of every web page visited, all instant messages sent, every email, every file sent or received and every web search entered. This is a trend that fundamentally changes the way users will view internet activity, at least when using corporate systems, and it has implications for all firms doing business online.

Operational Cyber Security Risks

At the operational level the focus of cyber security is on preventing, mitigating, detecting, investigating and responding to cyber-attacks. The richness and complexity of cyber-space means that there is a potentially endless list of attack scenarios, so we have attempted to group them into a few basic categories. The attack categories you are exposed to will inform you about the scale and sophistication of possible events, thus justifying your investment in countermeasures, while your analysis of the attack tools likely to be used will determine the operational and technical parameters of your response.

Categories of Attack

Table 6.1 summarises some key classes of cyber security attack by source or attacker type:

Table 6.1   Categories of cyber attack

Attack Category	Summary Description
State-sponsored attacks	These are increasingly frequent events involving attacks by state-funded or backed operations against the cyber-infrastructure of other states, non-state criminal or terrorist organisations, corporations or individuals of interest (business leaders, politicians, anti-government activists).
Asymmetrical warfare by non-state actors	This refers to so-called 'al-Qaeda style' cyber-warfare operations directed against a state or against individuals and corporations on the basis of their perceived alignment with a particular state or ideology.
Corporate espionage	This long-standing problem occurs when secret company data is stolen and passed to competitors. Though traditionally viewed as a hacking threat, we believe that the majority of these cases are internal in nature, involving employees or contractors of the targeted business.
Criminal attacks	This refers to cyber-attacks where the motive is not ideological or personal, but theft-related, though this may include attempts to delete or alter incriminating data, or to plant false evidence to incriminate an innocent party.
Anarchist attacks	Not to be discounted, the anarchist movement which flourished during the early part of the twentieth century is alive and well on the internet. Anarchy is not a nihilistic belief in the destruction of everything, but rather a commitment to the destruction of centralised authority, as represented by governments, large corporations and those who work with them. Anarchists can therefore wear many labels and they may not always be recognised for what they are.

It is also important to note the distinction between categories of cyber-attack and the attack tools listed in the following section.

Attack Tools

As cyber-technology evolves, the number of tools available for launching cyber-attacks also increases. Countermeasures have had to become increasingly sophisticated, which in turn means that the attackers have upped their own game, making for a complex, evolving situation and a long list of possible attack techniques, a number of which are often used in tandem. Table 6.2 below provides short descriptions of the most common attack tools.

Table 6.2   Common cyber security attack tools

Attack Tool	Summary Description
Computer Viruses	Small software programs that are replicated across multiple computer systems through user actions and which then execute an unwanted process. These may be malicious or benign. Infections can occur in a variety of ways, such as clicking on a link and downloading a file, using an infected USB memory stick, or as attachments to email.
Internet Worms	Similar to viruses but self-replicating and able to send themselves to other machines on a network without user intervention. One instance we saw recently was designed to detect all devices on a network and then send details back to a central point, probably as the basis for a more damaging subsequent cyber security attack.
Trojan Horses	A 'trojan' is a non-replicating piece of malware that appears to perform a useful function, but which actually facilitates unauthorised access to a user's systems and data.
Spyware	Spyware takes a number of forms, but is generally intended to monitor user activity, often for marketing purposes or to capture confidential data. Key loggers are a form of spyware that record all keystrokes made by a user in order to capture passwords, bank details, etc. Spyware is often installed on computers by internet Worms or via hidden downloads when a user browses to a malicious site.
Botnets	It has been estimated that 25 per cent of PCs worldwide are connected to a Botnet without their user's knowledge. A Botnet is a network of computers controlled by malware that has been installed by one of the means above. A remote controller will use the resources of this network of computers to carry out potentially malicious activities such as denial of service attacks against other systems, or to inflate traffic to other destinations in order to generate fraudulent revenue.
SQL Injection	Web-facing applications often store user name and password combinations, sometimes along with other sensitive data, in tables that are queried whenever a log on is attempted through the web interface. In certain cases, even major corporate firms have left themselves vulnerable to an attack based on entering ('injecting') SQL or other commands in place of user names and passwords. Such commands can extract the user name and password tables or access other confidential data.
Denial of Service (DoS)	DoS attacks typically involve flooding a target computer system with messages (e.g. email) in order to cause it to stop working.

Table 6.2   Continued

Attack Tool	Summary Description
Distributed DoS	This refers to an exploit wherein a network of computers, possibly controlled by a Botnet, floods the target computer with messages at the same time. This approach makes the attack harder to distinguish from legitimate high traffic.
Phishing	This refers to attempts to obtain secret data, such as passwords or bank and credit card details, from unsuspecting users by send fake messages that appear to come from credible sources, such as trusted websites, bank employees, system administrators, etc. Phishing is a form of 'social engineering' intended to facilitate unauthorised access to systems or fraud.
Pharming	Pharming attacks redirect traffic away from a legitimate website toward a false site. This is commonly done in order to obtain secret data from visitors without having to setup a Phishing scam.
URL Spoofing	URL spoofing refers to techniques used to edit the details of a URL displayed in a user's web browser in order to conceal a Pharming attack. The user may not be able to detect the fact that they have been directed away from a legitimate site simply by examining the URL.
IP Spoofing	This typically occurs during DoS attacks and refers to changes made to the attacker's IP address in order to conceal their identity.
Email Spoofing	This instance of spoofing refers to the editing of the 'From' field in an email message to hide the true identity of the sender, generally as part of a Phishing attack or fraud event.
Blackmail	Often ignored by technically minded people, the use of the internet as a way of delivered blackmail messages is very important. When combined with spoofing, a blackmailer can avoid detection while targeting an individual or organisation. Real time instructions, images and data can be included in such correspondence.

Primary Targets for Cyber-Attacks

Many of the critical infrastructures and commercial targets for cyber security attacks were once targets of the Allied strategic bombing campaign during World War II. They were recognised at that time to be critical to the cohesion and economic survival of a nation. Now, they are all connected to a shared global communications network which can be accessed by friends and potential enemies alike.

Cyber-security is a national security issue that should be of equal concern to both the public and private sectors. In our complex, interconnected world, no private company of significance can consider itself completely immune or isolated from the risk of cyber-attack by either state or non-state actors.

Interconnectedness and Cascading Failures

An estimated 90 per cent of internet infrastructure sits within the private sector, yet for private sector employees, as well as the general public, cyber-security awareness is still minimal. This situation is actually deteriorating in some respects, as corporate policies and guidelines fail to keep up with internet evolution and as more users come online, many having progressively lower levels of training and education.

A chain is only as strong as its weakest link and, in internet terms, the weakest link is the lax user. Given the extent to which we are all now interconnected and the potential for cascading failures across multiple sectors, business should be far more motivated to ensure that security and redundancy are guaranteed. As I write this, the RBS Group, which includes NatWest Bank, is entering a second week of chaos resulting from what has been described as a major technical computer failure. Whether this results from internal technical issues, or whether it was caused by a cyber security incident is unclear. The effect these events are having on the bank's brand and on its customers is nevertheless very severe and it would be the same regardless of the root cause of the problems.

However, even the basics such as password management, account deactivation on departure from the job, access controls, activity logging, control over data going off-site and ICT security audits are still weak across many sectors. Cyber security is a business continuity risk and it needs to be governed holistically, with both a mandate from and the focus of senior managers. We are all now utterly dependent on ICT and cyber technologies for business and commerce. Senior leaders must now get to grips with the details and include planning for cyber security in their strategic deliberations.

Penetration Testing

One of the main tools used to combat ICT security and cyber crime risks is Penetration Testing. Everyone has heard about it, but what is it really?

The main threats to these systems today are system intrusions, application exploits, denial of service attacks and malware. This section describes some of the activities and outcomes encompassed by security testing designed to identify and correct vulnerabilities to these increasingly sophisticated attacks.

THE PRINCIPLES OF NETWORK PENETRATION TESTING

A Network Penetration Test covers all of the key components in any ICT network. The most common types of test include:

- Router Testing

- Firewall Testing

- Intrusion Detection Testing

- Denial of Service Testing

- Database Testing

- Web Application Testing

- Perimeter System Testing

- Password Cracking

- Wireless Network Testing

RECONNAISSANCE

A network reconnaissance serves as an introduction to the systems to be tested. This step combines several activities such as data collection, information gathering and policy control. Additional hosts are often detected during actual testing and these new hosts may be inserted into the test plan as a subset of the pre-defined testing.

The expected results of this activity are:

- Port scanning

- OS/service fingerprinting

- Internet reconnaissance

- Online database searches

- IP and network reconnaissance

- Registrar and who-is searches

- Network Registry searches (ARIN)

- DNS reconnaissance

- Possible test limitations

VULNERABILITY ASSESSMENT

The objective of a vulnerability assessment is to identify, understand and verify weaknesses, configuration errors and vulnerabilities within a host or network. This involves searching online databases and mailing lists specific to the systems and network being tested. Searching is not confined to the web and IRC, newsgroups, and underground FTP sites are also searched.

Testing for vulnerabilities using automated tools is an efficient way to determine existing holes and system patch level. It is also important to identify and incorporate current underground scripts/exploits into this testing. However, manual verification is necessary for eliminating false positives, expanding the hacking scope, and discovering the data flow in and out of the network.

The typical results of this activity are:

- Types of application or service are mapped by vulnerability

- Patch levels of systems and applications are confirmed

- A list of possible denial of service vulnerabilities

- A list of areas secured by obscurity

- Lists of actual vulnerabilities with false positives removed

- Lists of vulnerabilities by system and application type

- Lists of internal or DMZ systems

- Lists of mail, server, and other naming conventions

- Network mapping

NETWORK LINKS AND PROTOCOL VULNERABILITY TESTING

Vulnerabilities occur not only in systems but also in the network communication links and during user interactions. During this phase of testing, communication links and vulnerable protocols are tested and potential security threats are identified. This analysis can capture traffic in transit such as emails, plain text passwords and files.

The expected results of this activity are:

- Identification of clear text communication paths in the network

- Detection of usernames and passwords that may be intercepted by attackers

- Flagging of confidential files in transit

- Flagging of confidential emails in transit

AUTOMATED MULTIPLE ATTACK VECTOR ANALYSIS

It is impossible to manually discover all possible attack paths and some may go unnoticed. Automated penetration testing tools can also be used to comprehensively determine all potential paths of attacks based on the system vulnerabilities.

EXPLOITATION

The exploitation process involves the creation of programs which can amend the proof of concept code in order to alter the normal flow of the target application by providing certain privileges to the penetration tester, which under normal circumstances would not have been present.

These exploit programs are broken down into three components:

- Network component

- Buffer creation component

- Payload component

The Network Component

This consists of libraries implementing the networking protocol through which the penetration test is launched.

The Buffer Creation Component

The most important part of an exploit program is the buffer creation component in which a penetration tester prepares a malformed request for triggering the vulnerability in the target application. This phase requires advanced analytical and debugging skills on the part of the tester.

The Payload Component

The payload component involves choosing the appropriate code that, when executed under the scope of the exploited application, will give the desired privilege to the tester. Once a working exploit is developed that is able to execute code on the local test setup, the exploit program is improved further to use universal return/overwrite addresses so that the exploit works irrespective of Operating System version and Service Packs.

SCENARIO MODELING ANALYSIS

Using what-if-analysis phase, different scenarios are simulated incrementally performing one change after another. 'What If' analysis is performed by designating one set of nodes as malicious attacker nodes and another set as target critical systems nodes and automatically determining all possible attack paths. The result of this activity provides a clear, prioritised list of vulnerabilities.

Some examples of the approaches taken are:

- Specify the threat origins (as an external attacker would) and critical targets (such as web servers) and regenerate the attack graph

- Mitigate certain vulnerabilities on targets in scan scope and again regenerate the attack graph.

- Change the routing rules and firewall ACL configurations and regenerate the attack graph

ROOT CAUSE ANALYSIS

After every test a root cause analysis must be conducted to confirm the existence and cause of critical vulnerabilities. This facilitates both the removal of the threat, as well as the prevention of similar occurrences in the future.

This post-mortem also helps to refine the test strategy so as to improve quality and performance in future. Many common security problems can be prevented proactively by maintaining security awareness in the planning and design stages of network engineering. Others may be a result of poor operational practice (perhaps due to network administration lacking focus on security). Identifying the root causes of the vulnerabilities discovered in a network allows patterns of vulnerabilities to be identified so that proactive prevention can be built into the business process.

RISK ASSESSMENT

A risk assessment is the first step in any risk control process and no network penetration test is complete without one. For vulnerabilities found, a risk calculation should be carried out to produce an assessment of the business impact in terms of financial loss and other costs.

The following methodology is recommended:

- Build user scenarios and derive use cases from them

- Create a network overview starting from use scenarios and use cases

- Analyse the technical backgrounds of the use cases

- Identify the assets in the use cases:

- Identify potential threats
- List the proven threats
- Determine the threat name, origin, entry points, assets and result
- Extract the fundamental threats from the threat scenarios
- Determine the likelihood of a threat trying to compromise a system using a specific threat scenario

• Identify vulnerabilities:

- Determine the vulnerabilities in each threat scenario
- Determine the likelihood of a vulnerability being exploited

• Risk Assessment:

- Determine the risk a threat poses based on asset value, frequency of occurrence, probability of detection, exploit likelihood and severity level
- Determine the best way to attach values to risk (quantitative)

PRINCIPLES OF APPLICATION PENETRATION TESTING

Application security risks can be defined as the pathways through your applications by which attackers may travel in order to cause a technical or business (operational, commercial or legal) impact on your organisation.

The OWASP Top 10

The current top 10 web-facing application risks (updated in 2010) defined by OWASP are summarised in Table 6.3, below.

Table 6.3   The OWASP top ten

#	Name	Description
A1	Injection	Injection flaws, such as SQL, OS, and LDAP injection, occur when un-trusted data is sent to an interpreter as part of a command or query. The attacker's hostile data can trick the interpreter into executing unintended commands or accessing unauthorised data.
A2	Cross-site scripting	XSS flaws occur whenever an application takes un-trusted data and sends it to a web browser without proper validation and escaping. XSS allows attackers to execute scripts in the victim's browser which can hijack user sessions, deface websites, or redirect the user to malicious sites.

Table 6.3   Continued

#	Name	Description
A3	Broken authentication and session management	Application functions related to authentication and session management are often not implemented correctly, allowing attackers to compromise passwords, keys, session tokens, or exploit other implementation flaws to assume other users' identities.
A4	Insecure direct object references	A direct object reference occurs when a developer exposes a reference to an internal implementation object, such as a file, directory, or database key. Without an access control check or other protection, attackers can manipulate these references to access unauthorised data.
A5	Cross-site request forgery	A CSRF attack forces a logged-on victim's browser to send a forged HTTP request, including the victim's session cookie and any other automatically included authentication information, to a vulnerable web application. This allows the attacker to force the victim's browser to generate requests the vulnerable application thinks are legitimate requests from the victim.
A6	Security misconfiguration	Good security requires having a secure configuration defined and deployed for the application, frameworks, application server, web server, database server, and platform. All these settings should be defined, implemented, and maintained as many are not shipped with secure defaults. This includes keeping all software up to date, including all code libraries used by the application.
A7	Insecure cryptographic storage	Many web applications do not properly protect sensitive data, such as credit cards, SSNs, and authentication credentials, with appropriate encryption or hashing. Attackers may steal or modify such weakly protected data to conduct identity theft, credit card fraud, or other crimes.
A8	Failure to restrict URL access	Many web applications check URL access rights before rendering protected links and buttons. However, applications need to perform similar access control checks each time these pages are accessed, or attackers will be able to forge URLs to access these hidden pages anyway.
A9	Insufficient transport layer protection	Applications frequently fail to authenticate, encrypt, and protect the confidentiality and integrity of sensitive network traffic. When they do, they sometimes support weak algorithms, use expired or invalid certificates, or do not use them correctly.
A10	Unvalidated redirects and forwards	Web applications frequently redirect and forward users to other pages and websites, and use un-trusted data to determine the destination pages. Without proper validation, attackers can redirect victims to phishing or malware sites, or use forwards to access unauthorised pages.

Note: See www.owasp.org/index.php/Category:OWASP_Top_Ten_Project

The following sections summarise the main application penetration tests that should be covered, as per the current OWASP guidelines.

Information Gathering

Information disclosure covers attacks designed to acquire system specific information about a website. System specific information includes the software distribution, version numbers and patch levels. Most websites will reveal a certain amount of data, but it is best to limit the amount of data whenever possible. The more information about the website an attacker learns, the easier the system becomes to compromise.

The following tests are recommended:

- Spiders, robots and crawlers

- Search engine discovery/reconnaissance

- Identify application entry points

- Testing web application fingerprint

- Application discovery

- Analysis of error codes

Configuration Testing

Testing against the server and application configuration may reveal sensitive information regarding the infrastructure and topology in place. This information may vary from simple HTTP methods being used to revealing critical information related to encryption/cryptology flows.

Some key forms of testing included in configuration management are:

- SSL/TLS testing

- DB listener testing

- Infrastructure configuration management testing

- Application configuration management testing

- Testing for file extensions handling

- Old, backup and unreferenced files

- Infrastructure and application admin interfaces

- Testing for HTTP methods and XST

Business Logic Testing

Logical attacks focus on the abuse or exploitation of a web application's logic flow. Application logic is the expected procedural flow used in order to perform a certain action. Password recovery, account registration, auction bidding and e-commerce purchases are all examples of application logic. A website may require a user to correctly perform a specific multi-step process to complete a particular action. An attacker may be able to circumvent or misuse these features to harm a website and its users.

Authentication Testing

Authentication testing targets a website's method of validating the identity of a user, service or application. Authentication is performed using at least one of three mechanisms: 'something you have', 'something you know' or 'something you are'. Two factor authentication, for example, would require you to authenticate against two of these categories (e.g. a biometric scan *plus* a password you have memorised).

An assessment of the common vulnerabilities exploited to circumvent the authentication process of a standard website should include:

- Analysis of credentials transported over an encrypted channel

- User enumeration testing

- Guessable (Dictionary) user account testing

- Brute force testing

- Authentication scheme bypassing test

- 'Remember Password', 'Password Reset' and weak password recovery validation testing

- Logout and browser cache management testing

- CAPTCHA (or similar human verification) testing

- Multiple factors authentication testing

- Race conditions testing

- Insufficient authentication testing

Authorisation Testing

Authorisation testing targets a website's method of determining if a user, service or application has the necessary permissions to perform a requested action. For example, many websites should only allow certain users to access specific content or functionality. At other times a user's access to other resources might be restricted. Using various techniques, listed below, an attacker can fool a website into increasing their privileges to protected areas and all of these should be tested and assessed:

- Path traversal

- Authorisation scheme bypass

- Privilege escalation

- Credential/Session prediction

- Insufficient authorisation

- Insufficient session expiration

- Session fixation

Client-side Attacks

Client-side attack assessments focus on the abuse or exploitation of a website's users. When a user visits a website, trust is established between the two parties both technologically and psychologically. A user expects websites they visit to deliver valid content. A user also expects the website not to attack them during their stay. By leveraging these trust relationship expectations, an attacker may employ several techniques to exploit the user and testing is required to establish the exposure of clients to each of these:

- Content spoofing testing

- Cross-site scripting testing

  - Testing for reflected cross-site scripting

  - Testing for stored cross-site scripting

  - Testing for DOM based cross-site scripting

  - Testing for cross-site flashing

Data Validation Testing

The most common web application security weakness is the failure to properly validate input coming from the client or environment before using it. This weakness leads to almost all of the major vulnerabilities in web applications, such as cross site scripting, SQL injection, interpreter injection, locale/Unicode attacks, file system attacks and buffer overflows.

Data from an external entity or client should never be trusted, since it can be arbitrarily tampered with by an attacker. Complex applications often have a large number of entry points, which makes it difficult for a developer to enforce this rule. Data validation testing is the task of testing all the possible forms of input, to understand if the application sufficiently validates input data before using it.

Session Management Testing

HTTP is a stateless protocol, and is unable to track users against a request, so this functionality is generally achieved by writing a logical piece of code which is termed as a 'session'. The session helps the web application to track users and his/her controls to perform specific operations right from authentication until the user leaves the application. In case of mismanagement of a session, the users might suffer from data/information loss. The following tests are generally conducted to ensure that proper session management is in place:

- Session management scheme testing

- Cookie attributes testing

- Session fixation testing

- Exposed session variables testing

- CSRF (Cross Site Request Forgery) testing

- HTTP Exploit testing

Denial of Service Testing

A Denial of Service attack is an attempt to interrupt the legitimate users to avail the services offered by application/server. In terms of web applications, an attacker may be able to accomplish a partial or complete Denial of Service, thus making several functions or even complete services unavailable or unusable. Tests that should be performed to check against Denial of Service Vulnerability include:

- Testing for SQL wildcard attacks

- DoS testing: locking customer accounts

- DoS testing: buffer overflows

- DoS testing: user specified object allocation

- DoS testing: user input as a loop counter

- DoS testing: writing user provided data to disk

- DoS testing: failure to release resources

- DoS testing: storing too much data in session

Web Services Testing

Web servers provide various valuable services across the globe, but are exposed over the internet and are accessible to many users. Web servers, just as in the case of applications, are also vulnerable to several vulnerabilities such as SQL injection and information/data leakage vulnerabilities, along with several web server specific vulnerabilities. The following tests must be performed to verify web server vulnerability:

- WS information gathering

- Testing WSDL

- XML structural testing

- XML content-level testing

- HTTP GET parameters/REST testing

- Naughty SOAP attachments

- Replay testing

Ajax Testing

Ajax is one of the latest web development techniques to create more advanced and responsive web applications. Though the usability of AJAX provides many valuable features, it also widens the range of vulnerabilities if it is not designed or developed properly. The conventional web application vulnerabilities described above are all applicable to AJAX based development, as are several specific vulnerabilities such as Cross Site request forgery (CSRF/XSRF).

Network and application penetration testing is an increasingly important and increasingly complex practice area. Not only must your testers possess the technical skills required to execute this task, but they must have the personal qualities essential for you to be able to trust in them and their work. TRMG supplies state-of-the-art penetration testing services to business and government, using the highest calibre ethical testing engineers and tools.

Social Media and Fraud

In late 2010, concerned about an increase in the number of burglaries being facilitated by social engineering of victims via Facebook, insurers Legal & General conducted a survey[1] to assess the willingness of people in the UK to share personal data with strangers online. The results were startling. 59 per cent of men and 42 per cent of women surveyed admitted that they had accepted friend requests from strangers on Facebook based solely on liking the other

---

1   See www.legalandgeneral.com/_resources/pdfs/insurance/digital-criminal-2.pdf

person's photo. 13 per cent of men and 9 per cent of women had shared their phone numbers via Facebook and 9 per cent (men) and 4 per cent (women) had posted their home address.

As concern about vulnerabilities on Facebook and similar social media services grew during 2011, the University of British Colombia conducted its own experiment,[2] launching 100 fake profiles which generated 5,000 friend requests to test user's willingness to 'friend' strangers. According to the UBC report, 19 per cent (596 users) accepted this first round of requests. The fake accounts then targeted the friends of the 19 per cent and on this occasion 59 per cent (2,079) of those invited to 'friend' accepted.

While the Legal & General survey focused on the importance of attractiveness the UBC study addresses the principle of Triadic Closure – you are more likely to accept a request of friendship from me if I am already a friend of a friend. At TRMG we decided to conduct our own tests, fabricating five Facebook accounts, four with pretty female profiles and one with a Neanderthal image and name. Within a week the female profiles each had up to 140 Facebook friends. By friending and recommending the Neanderthal account, the fake female accounts were then able to find 45 friends willing to link with it, despite it clearly being a fake profile. One further factor was that the Neanderthal account would often 'like' photos and comments posted by others, leading some to offer friendship voluntarily.

From this research we concluded that the combination of triadic closure, attractiveness and liking represents a valuable tool for those with malicious or criminal intent. We have developed some scenarios in which criminals might profit from this.

KEY SOCIAL ENGINEERING AND FRAUD RISKS

- *Targeting*: LinkedIn, Facebook and others offer excellent sources of targeting information for criminals. Many users post their locations, sometimes updating these automatically. Travel plans are included via services such as Tripit and Trip Advisor.

- *Identity theft and impersonation*: not only are real names and photos displayed, but email addresses, phone numbers, children's

---

2   See http://lersse-dl.ece.ubc.ca/record/264/files/ACSAC_2011.pdf

names and even dates of birth are regularly included in public profiles.

- *Data disclosure*: as demonstrated by a senior UK politician recently, social media provides a mechanism for broadcasting confidential data to the whole planet. The politician apologised after he admitted to tipping off a journalist about an embarrassing story involving a competitor in a public tweet that was intended to be.[3]

- *Market distortion via fake profiles*: setting up a fake Facebook profile is child's play and impersonation of senior figures, or even the creation of fake company pages is equally straightforward. By putting out inaccurate market information in order to trade with an advantage, a fraudster could potentially distort the market with minimal risk of being detected.

- *Reputational harm and blackmail*: by exploiting the attractiveness principle a would-be blackmailer can execute a 'honey trap attack' on a target, enticing him or her to say or do things that would be harmful if exposed.

- *'Nigerian 419 frauds'*: these attacks still occur and social media offers a potential goldmine to those wishing to more effectively adapt their 419 messages to their targets.

OPEN SOURCE SOCIAL MEDIA MONITORING OPPORTUNITIES

Like fashion, social media provides an unprecedented open source monitoring opportunity for crime fighting and fraud prevention. Examples of the types of fraud that can be detected through monitoring of social media feeds include:

- Benefits fraud

- Insurance fraud

- Fraudulent sick leave claims

- Social engineering investigations

---

3   See www.independent.co.uk/news/uk/politics/chris-huhne-admits-twitter-gaffe-was-linked-to
    -catflap-affair-2368108.html

Due diligence research for anti-money laundering and other financial assessments (to assess politically exposed persons, for example) also benefit hugely from social media monitoring.

Open source monitoring tools come in two main flavours. A majority of these tools have their roots in the marketing industry and they consequently focus on high level analysis of sentiment and usage. Arguably, the more effective approach from a digital intelligence perspectiveinvolves targeted monitoring of named accounts, conducted in an ethical manner.

Open source monitoring is not a substitute for traditional intelligence and investigative techniques; rather it provides an additional stream of data that can reveal personal information about criminals and their associates that would not otherwise have been available.

Open Source Social Media Monitoring Risks

Any investigator embarking on social media open source intelligence ('OSINT') activities is advised to consider the risks very carefully. Foremost among these is the mistake of confusing intelligence with evidence. While the courts may not yet recognise the weaknesses inherent in data gathered from social media sites, this must surely change as time passes. There is an increasing awareness that the complete absence of identity verification and the apparently ineffective nature of the security mechanisms employed by sites like Facebook means that 'evidence' gathered from such sources is more and more likely to be contested. Indeed, retrospective reviews of cases that depended on such evidence may one day be necessary.

There are also serious ethical considerations to bear in mind. The creation of a fake profile that leads to a conversation with the subject may represent entrapment in some circumstances. Clear legal guidelines are essential and RIPA principles will always apply for public sector organisations. Privacy settings are available to all social media users and we always recommend that OSINT investigators respect these asanything that lies behind the wall of a privacy setting is *not* open source.

In conclusion, our approach to social media OSINT is captured in this simple list:

Do

- Capture genuine open source data

- Analyse content for evidence of criminal behaviour, links, incitement, deception or intent

- Use open source data as intelligence to guide other enquiries

Don't

- Operate in cowboy mode, without clear guidelines

- Use fake profiles to get suspects to say things they wouldn't otherwise have said

- Attempt to access private data and conversations without a supporting legal opinion

- Blindly use data gathered from social media sites as evidence

7

Other Risk Management Considerations

Calculating the Return on Investment

Many fraud and revenue assurance teams find it very difficult to demonstrate their return on investment to the business and they therefore struggle to justify headcounts and spending on fraud and RA control technologies. In this section we provide a few key insights into ways in which we have seen clients avoid this particular pitfall.

As the early adopters of advanced fraud and revenue assurance applications move beyond the implementation stage of the revenue risk control lifecycle into the operational stage, the question of return on investment becomes ever more sensitive. A significant proportion of those who have invested heavily in large teams and expensive solutions are still struggling to demonstrate a positive return on that investment, while others are storming ahead and kicking off new projects in cost assurance, tariff assurance and settlements.

What differentiates these two groups and what can operators who are considering an investment in fraud or RA learn from the lessons of the past few years?

FOUR KEY GUIDELINES

Our experience with operators suggests four guidelines for a financially successful revenue risk control programme:

- Manage project sponsor and senior management expectations

- Walk before you run by taking a careful step-by-step approach to the project

- Test the business case for each control and factor recovery cost erosion into this analysis

- Adopt a risk-based approach and address your top risks first – trifling risks need not be managed

Managing the Sponsor's Expectations

RA and fraud managers are often caught between a rock and a hard place. On the one hand, senior management sponsorship is hard to come by and internal competition for top management attention is tough. If you want to secure the funding for your programme, you may feel that you have to do two things:

1. Produce an estimate of fraud or revenue loss that is dramatic enough to worry stakeholders

2. Predict fraud savings or revenue loss recoveries that will make a contribution to corporate revenues large enough to warrant investment

You will also talk about governance, compliance and due diligence, but everyone knows that it's fraud losses, revenue leakage and savings or recoveries that will win the day.

But beware; the revenue recovery figures you cite today will return to haunt you a year from now. Make sure you really do know what you are talking about and factor in the likelihood that once the 'low hanging fruit' has been harvested your incremental recoveries will diminish rapidly. Set the sponsor's expectations accordingly as not enough budget is always better than unrealistic performance targets.

Walking Before You Run

Revenue risk management projects are exciting. You are going to challenge the corporate orthodoxy, find lost monies and demonstrate weaknesses in business processes and platforms. You're going to be a corporate hero.

However, whether you are charging actual dragons or merely attacking windmills, it's a good idea to advance on only one of these objects at a time. Pick an easy one to start with, one with well documented data types and formats, available data feeds and, preferably, lots of known issues.

In most cases, what you thought would be straightforward will turn out to be more costly and complex than expected, but you will now be far better able to assess the risks and rewards of the next phase of your project *before* committing to it.

Testing the Business Case for Each Control

We shudder when we see an a fraud or RA team kicking off a vast measurement project with 50 control points and 100 types of reconciliation or report. What is their business case? How will they manage change? Where do their priorities lie? There must be a better way and there is.

Test the business case for each and every control before you formally propose it. The most effective way to do this is to take data samples and conduct your tests with them:

- How easy was it to obtain the sample data?

- Was it in a usable format?

- Will you need technical support from your vendor to read these files?

- What will that vendor support cost?

- Will you need all the data or only some of it?

- How often will you need to extract it?

- How long will you store it?

- How much disk space and processing time will the data demand?

- By how much will your total system costs increase?

- How much staff effort will be required to process and analyse this data routinely?

- What evidence of leakage or fraud was found during the test?

- Is there other evidence of leakage or fraud related to the revenue stream in question?

- How much of the leakage or fraud found could be recovered or prevented in reality?

- What would an ongoing fraud prevention or revenue leakage recovery activity cost the business?

- Would the business have found this fraud or leakage anyway, without your input?

- *Is there a clear business case for this control?*

Adopting a Risk-Based Approach

A risk-based approach is a methodology for assessing business and financial risks, and scoring them using selected criteria in order to prioritise treatment and support effective decision making.

In Telecoms Fraud and RA operations, the main criteria for assessing revenue risks are:

- *Environmental risks*: is revenue risk a characteristic of the operating environment (e.g. recessionary pressures)?

- *Technology risks*: is the technology deployed inherently risky or open to attack (e.g. IP infrastructure)?

- *Business process risks*: are the firm's business processes a major source of risk (e.g. lack of credit vetting, extensive bill recycling, etc.)?

- *People risks*: are subscriber or employee risks known to be a significant factor (e.g. fraud and bad debt)?

The concept of a risk-based approach is very simple – you focus your finite resources on the risks that have the greatest frequency and impact on the business. When applied to fraud and RA, this essentially means that you must assess the financial business case for each control, consider the frequency of loss events addressed by the control, weigh any other factors such as reputational or compliance risks, and then propose a tailored programme that prioritises the top-scoring risks and applies diminishing levels or frequency of monitoring to those risks appearing lower down the scale. In general, this is done sequentially by revenue stream, with the highest revenue generating streams being addressed first, because their size infers higher levels of risk.

A risk-based approach dictates that the allocation of resources (people, tools and budgets) to deal with manifest or anticipated risks, should be done on the basis of a holistic assessment of risk. What this essentially means is that revenue risks should not be assessed in terms of operational 'silos' (i.e. fraud, RA and credit being viewed as separate items) but as a single list of risks.

Resource and budgetary allocations should be directed at the risks with the greatest business impact. In other words, credit may get 50 per cent of the total risk control budget allocation this year, with expert telecoms risk people from other teams being moved across to focus on that area, while next year it may be determined that revenue leakage should be given priority.

This calls for cross-training, matrix management and consolidated reporting to support sensible decision making. Structured risk reviews are a common means of assessing the organisation's posture in this regard.

Ideally, such a review will be regularly repeated in order to assess the need for change, but an effectively managed risk-based approach serves to save your business money while ensuring that the activities you do undertake deliver the best possible value.

ASSESSING AND EXPLAINING IMPACTS

The key stakeholders in terms of fraud and revenue assurance are many and revenue loss has impacts that go beyond the purely financial to include accuracy of reporting, regulatory compliance, cost assurance, brand value and shareholder value.

Fraud and RA managers need to consider the full list of stakeholders in order to tailor their plans and prioritise issues based on a broader set of decision criteria than mere financial write-offs.

For example, an issue of personal data exposure may be more significant in brand and regulatory terms than a $1 million fraud loss, but the organisation may not have a method for modelling the impact of such intangibles and the fraud manager will need to assess this independently.

Stakeholders typically have demands on RA and fraud that fall into two categories:

Loss Prevention

Stakeholders want revenue loss to be prevented. Where it cannot be prevented, they want it to be quickly detected, investigated and mitigated. They then want future incidents to be prevented through process re-engineering or technical counter measures.

Reporting

Stakeholders want to know about losses that have occurred before the press and the market hear about them. They want the information reported to be complete, accurate and timely.

Stakeholders look to RA and fraud to provide an assurance that both of these expectations can and will be met by the operating business units.

The Controls Assessment

The team must understand and score the controls in place and/or needed to address each manifest risk. These are often maintained in a Risk Register that is updated monthly and shared with the Risk Committee.

Managers will invariably find it challenging to assess the effectiveness of the business processes in place to control fraud and revenue leakage.However, there are a few simple indicators that provide a good picture of where improvements might be needed:

- *Leakage as a percentage of revenue*: if leakage is higher than industry norms (often quoted as 1–2 per cent of revenue, but varying widely by region and technology) a problem may exist.

- *Fraud as a percentage of bad debt*: this is commonly thought to be around 33 per cent, so high levels of debt suggest high levels of fraud. You will need to establish what the actual ratios are in your business before using this expression.

- *Bad debt trending*: again, if write-offs for debt are rising, undetected fraud may be rising too.

- *Ratio of time spent processing data versus time spent analysing data*: if employees are focused primarily on processing FMS and RA data, rather than analysing it, more effective automation is probably needed.

- *Case value trending*: if the value of incidents is rising, there is a need for remedial action.

The Operating Procedures Review

The team must review all operating procedures, as well as the supporting IT infrastructure, in order to score current practices against recommended best practice. The fraud or RA managershould perform the following analysis:

- *Gap analysis*: develop an understanding of the existing gaps between identified risks and established controls.

- *Estimate of financial exposure*: produce an estimate of the potential financial impact of risks that are not effectively controlled.

- *Assess costs, benefits and ROI*: produce an assessment of the costs and benefits of controls that could be introduced to address gaps identified and also examine the return on investment of existing controls.

- *Action plan*: produce a management report and proposed action plan, based on the above.

- *Follow-up*: ensure that the plan is agreed and executed.

The Gap Analysis

The purpose of a fraud or RA gap analysis is to:

- Provide a listing of all controls that satisfy the requirements imposed by best practice guidelines and management

- Provide a listing of open leakage or fraud issues identified

- Provide a description of all duplications and overlaps

- Provide a description of any gaps

- Submit recommendations for resolving the gaps and overlaps to the Risk Committee for review, approval and resolution

Effecting Change

The primary goal of these activities is to trigger change. Therefore, the fraud or RA manager must be able to communicate key findings and recommendations in a format that is easily understood by decision makers.

Communicating the case for change requires the manager to understand two key drivers for change in any business:

- Push factors

- Pull factors

PUSH FACTORS

Push factors are positive drivers that primarily influence organisations that aspire to market leadership. Senior managers in such firms will 'invest to be the best', and respond more positively to this kind of messaging.

PULL FACTORS

Pull factors are negative drivers that primarily influence organisations where a state of crisis is felt to exist. Firms that have suffered or are exposed to significant losses and firms that fear regulatory or other penalties are most likely to be responsive to this form of messaging.

The fraud and RA manager must understand his audience before submitting his recommendations for change.

ESTIMATING FINANCIAL IMPACTS

Revenue losses due to fraud and revenue leakage events have multi-faceted financial impacts. The fraud and RA manager must consider each of these when computing the total loss or exposure associated with any given risk.

- *Write-offs*: the sums considered irretrievably lost to the business and written off by Finance.

- *Investment loss*: an expression of how many dollars had to be invested to generate the revenue that has now been written off. You should normally seek assistance from Finance before attempting to compute this.

- *Deferred revenues*: inflows that are delayed by the fraud or leakage event (e.g. recycled billing events).

- *Opportunity costs*: revenue opportunities that have been missed and cannot be recovered (e.g. in cases of incorrect rating).

- *Recovery costs*: the cost of detecting, investigating and recovering revenue leakage or fraud losses.

- *Insurance costs*: the cost of insurance premiums in cases where these categories of loss are covered.

In addition to the direct financial exposure outlined on the previous page, the business is exposed to other impacts which may be harder to measure, but which are equally important:

- *Reputational damage*: public awareness of high levels of fraud or leakage, or of inaccurate billing can badly damage the brand.

- *Share price impact*: awareness can also affect the share price if confidence in the governance of the business is eroded.

- *Churn*: customers who are hit by fraud or over-billing may switch providers.

- *Regulatory penalties*: fines may be imposed by the regulator for poor governance or over-billing.

- *Infrastructure costs*: the total investment in infrastructure covers all traffic, including fraudulent traffic for which there is no revenue.

The assessment of the potential costs and benefits associated with revenue leakage risks and controls rests on a few additional criteria:

- *Cost of system acquisition*: the cost to procure, install and commission new technology.

- *Cost of system ownership*: the running costs (support, upgrades and licences) of each solution proposed.

- *Staff costs*: the headcount cost.

- *Other logistical costs*: office space etc.

- *Estimated total leakage*: the total value of leakage being addressed.

- *Potential recoveries as a percentage of leakage*: the potential for revenue recovery.

This estimate should also take into account the potential for revenue recovery through normal business processes. In many cases, the business would recover from a loss without specific fraud and RA interventions.

In order to assess the true return on investment (RoI) of any existing or proposed revenue risk management control or initiative, the following *Revenue Recovery Erosion* factors must be taken into account:

- *Cost of correction*: the cost of fixing leakage issues operationally.

- *Cost of recovery*: the cost of chasing fraud losses through the courts or recycling billing, etc.

- *Unrecoverable revenues*: what is the amount of leakage that can never be recovered? (Recovery will almost never be 100 per cent.)

- *Unrecovered revenues*: what is the value of leakage that remains uncovered, but which could potentially be recovered? (This is the remaining recovery opportunity and is central to your business case for the next period.)

- *Rebates and penalties*: will refunds or penalties need to be paid in relation to the specific type of leakage event?

THE ACTION PLAN

Weaknesses and gaps must be addressed by an agreed plan for remedial actions, signed off with the steering group. The task of defining the RA and Fraud Risk control plans should follow a systematic process to ensure that all fundamental business aspects and IT-service support activities are understood and considered. Therefore, it is essential that the foundation of the plan is rooted in the organisation's objectives, strategies and business model.

The first step in defining the plan is to understand the business. As part of this step, managers need to identify the strategies, objectives, key performance indicators and business models that will enable them to understand the organisation's unique business risks. The team also needs to understand how existing business operations and IT service functions support the fraud and RA organisation.

TEAM RESOURCING STRATEGIES

A first step is to estimate the available Fraud, RA and IT resources for the project. This requires the creation of a Technical Skills Inventory that is mapped against the management plan. The availability of resources is established and a plan for the provision of additional resources, along with a proposed budget, is put before the steering group for review.

Board, senior management and regulatory requests included in the plan which are related to specific areas of interest should be highlighted. Revenue assurance and fraud management commonly follows three parallel tracks:

Benchmarking and KPI Measurement

This takes the form of assessments of current business practices against a set of best practice guidelines, and is conducted along traditional review lines.

Internal Business Consulting

This involves the team giving advice to the operating departments in a consultancy model, particularly in new areas of risk where best practice models have not yet been developed.

Data Analytics

This requires the extraction of billing and platform data, often in large volumes, to facilitate the execution of analysis, either to validate the findings reported by the business, or to detect new areas of fraud risk or revenue leakage and to support investigations.

Teams are required to multi-task and to employ a mix of skills and techniques. The organisation's RA and Fraud control model will determine the IT function's structure and delivery model. For instance, companies operating with converged Fraud and RA teams may have converged IT platforms. Others may have more diversity of applications, and a larger variety of deployed products.

TYPES OF RISK FACTOR

There are three types of risk factor that are normally considered:

- *Subjective risk factors*: an experienced practitioner's sound subjective judgment is just as valid as any other method, and managers should take on board internal and external expertise in order to obtain this.

- *Objective or historical risk factors*: in all cases, current objective information is helpful in measuring risk. The client's own organisation is generally the best source of this information.

- *Calculated risk factors*: a subset of objective risk factor data is the class of factors calculated from actual sample data, often using portable analytics tools.

Based on the preceding assessment of risk factors, the management team can design and use an appropriate Risk Impact Model. The Risk Impact Model's scaling and ranking method needs to be adapted to suit the differing classes of Fraud, RA or IT risk identified, but Tables 7.1, 7.2 and 7.3 provide an example of how a simple model may be constructed.

Table 7.1   The likelihood scale

H	3	High probability that the risk will occur.
M	2	Medium probability that the risk will occur.
L	1	Low probability that the risk will occur.

Table 7.2   The impact scale

H	3	The potential for material impact on the organisation's earnings, assets, reputation or stakeholders is high.
M	2	The potential for material impact on the organisation's earnings, assets, reputation or stakeholders may be significant to the management unit, but moderate in terms of the whole organisation.
L	1	The potential for material impact on the organisation's earnings, assets, reputation or stakeholders is low.

As shown, a simple scoring method based on high, medium and low (3, 2, 1) scores can be used for the likelihood of occurrence or the impact of each manifested risk. This is based on the concepts presented previously. Impact assessment scoring may be based on past experience, assessments by subject matter experts, or on projections from data analytics and scenario-based testing.

Finally, the controls in place within the organisation need to be offset against the risks observed. A simple model for scoring controls seen is shown in Table 7.3. Risks in each area are scored by likelihood and impact and a risk score is derived.

Note that the controls score will be deducted from the risks score so that high risk minus high control level (3-3) equals a low final score. A simple risk controls analysis table allows the management team to score the controls already in place.

Table 7.3   Control scoring

H	3	The level of control in place to identify and mitigate known and suspected risks is high.
M	2	The level of control in place to identify and mitigate known and suspected risks is moderate.
L	1	The level of control in place to identify and mitigate known and suspected risks is low.

It is common to capture the controls in a separate worksheet, to group and number them, to include diagrams to illustrate the controls, and to then indicate the control score against each risk. The controls score is then deducted to produce a final risk score. This means that high risk areas with excellent levels of control will be treated as low scoring issues and the focus of the management team will be on areas of high risk in which poor controls were identified.

A simple risk vs. controls scoring table allows the management team to establish reasonable grounds for the prioritisation of specific areas of management focus and the development of a practical plan of action that is supported by a logical business case.

8

Other Strategic Risks

As we have suggested in the text, communications technology is part of the bedrock of modern social, economic and governmental life. Without it, most of the processes we depend on for our daily existence would simply cease to operate, leaving us all adrift and without any of the traditional manual alternatives to fall back on.

Communications and related ICT technologies form the 'technology' part of the people, processes and technology triangle, as it relates to strategic risk and national security. Two scenarios illustrate this very clearly, while also underscoring the effect that other forms of risk might have on the communications infrastructure. The first is a global food security crisis and the second is cyber warfare.

Food security, energy security, water security and cyber security are now paramount concerns for strategic thinkers worldwide. Not only climate change, but population growth, changing consumption patterns, the trailing off of the revolution in food production and the potential exhaustion of key fossil fuel resources all exacerbate the risks of food security crises and international conflicts leading to cyber warfare – the two events have a symbiotic relationship in the sense that the occurrence of either one would almost certainly trigger the other. Communications risk managers need to be aware of how the networks they oversee are simultaneously a critical dependency, an avenue of attack, and a target in their own right. In the post-privatisation era, therefore, ways need to be found to bring private firms into line with national security standards.

Global Food Security

Although global food production peaked in 2008 and food prices (indexed to wages) fell by 75 per cent between 1945 and that year, an estimated 1 billion people still go to bed hungry every night in the developing world. This last number, which declined by almost 20 per cent between 1970 and 1990, has now risen above its original 1970 level, partly due to population growth. Some 200,000 people are born every day, while average life expectancy is growing steadily in most countries. World population is consequently projected to grow by a further 34 per cent over the next four decades and already stands at 7 billion people today.[1]

Meanwhile, in the UK and many other advanced economies, supply chain management tools and techniques have been optimised to the point where 'just in time' delivery of supplies from around the world has almost eliminated the need for food storage. On the one hand, this is a hugely impressive achievement that ensures not only that warehouse capacity requirements (and therefore costs) are minimised, but also that the food delivered to consumers is now fresher than ever before.

On the other hand, our nations are dependent on a very finely tuned system that rests primarily on a single technology: communications. Take away the communications channels and the entire system fails. In the UK, the period of time during which existing stocks in transit will keep the nation fed is believed to be only a few days.

There are several possible scenarios in which such a communications failure might occur:

- Unrelated major network outage, possibly linked to an attack or to system failures

- A cyber attack deliberately targeting our food supply chain communications technologies (e.g. by a hostile state against whom we are conducting conventional military operations)

- A cyber or terrorist-style attack inspired by a global food security crisis and instigated or supported by a state that competes with us for food from the same sources

- Internal sabotage resulting from civil or industrial unrest linked to recessionary pressures

---

1   Peter Brabeck-Letmathe, Chairman, Nestle S.A. 2010.

Food security risk is consequently not an issue that can be ignored by communications risk managers as food, water, health pandemics, natural disasters and energy are among a group of risks that require cross-sector responses. Each risk management professional needs to keep abreast of the latest food security developments and likely future trends. Unfortunately, the fragility of the supply chain mechanisms now employed is compounded by other developments.

FOOD PRICES

Since the onset of the 2007/2008 recession, prices for all key foodstuffs started to rise, driven in large part by increasing demand from the likes of China and by major climate events, such as the drought and fires that ravaged Russia's wheat harvest. A projected global shortfall in water supply is expected to cause a corresponding shortfall in cereals production of 30 per cent over the next five years.[2] The impact of this on food supply and pricing is compounded by the increasing diversion of grain to bio fuels production, particularly in the USA.

While policy makers and economists worry about the impact of food scarcity on prices and national security, health and public unrest, risk managers should be thinking about the implications of these risks in terms of physical threats to staff and networks, as well as the resulting increases in the cost of insurance and security.

WATER SECURITY

Food security is inextricably linked to water security and inadequate water supply is not merely a local consideration. One area of focus for communications risk managers working anywhere in the food supply and distribution chain should be water supply at the point of production, as it is shortages there that will have the most obvious and immediate impact on the situation at the point of sale. Analysis of water supply risks must extend over the horizon, both geographically and metaphorically, to incorporate facts about the long-term dependability of supply location by location. In other words, the primary water supply risks for the risk manager of a major food distribution organisation sitting in London (and for the risk manager at the firm that supply his communications services) will be the water supply risks that farmers face in Russia, Kenya, Ecuador or Malaysia. The corporate risk manager needs to be in a position to alert senior decision-makers years in advance if water supply in

---

2   *Financial Times* 2010.

far flung but relevant places has the potential to limit production of a food or substantially increase costs.

OFFSHORE FOOD PRODUCTION

Regardless of where individuals stand on the debate between those who see climate change as primarily man-made and those who regard it as part of the natural cycle, climate shifts are already having a serious impact on food production. Several nations, including China, have started to move parts of their food producing activities offshore, buying huge tracts of land in fertile regions in Africa in order to produce food there exclusively for repatriation to the home country.

That such a hedge against food scarcity is considered necessary by a number of major players should be a warning to risk managers in any industry about their exposure to food crises. Consequently, an awareness of climate change trends and their anticipated impact on food production is essential.

Global food security is a strategic concern that has the potential to directly affect every risk management operation in every industry or sector. Nevertheless, it is one of the few key risks that can be forecast and monitored. A comprehensive plan to address the effects of food scarcity events and the related risks for communications infrastructure is something that every communications risk manager should consider. Essential points include:

- Which organisations are dependent on communications services from my business as essential facets of national food distribution channels?

- Have we put special service level agreements in place for these strategic clients?

- In the event of a crisis or network failure, do our contingency plans for providing continued service to key users adequately cover our national food supply chain network?

Cyber Warfare

In many of the numerous discussions and papers published over recent years that address the concept of cyber warfare, one key word often seems to be omitted – globalisation. Disentangling the globalised economy from the global internet is probably impossible and it is this single factor that makes a major cyber war involving the world's leading powers potentially catastrophic. The concept of economic mutually assured destruction (ECONMAD) is one that I have developed to describe this scenario. This is based on the MAD thinking that strategists developed during the Cold War.

The internet is a digital spider's web and national governments are the flies trapped in its sticky embrace, not quite understanding their predicament, but powerless to escape their bonds. The internet was created for the public sector, but it has been expanded and exploited primarily by the private. The divergence of national political goals and those of globalised corporate entities is nowhere evidenced more clearly than in the structure of the internet and the uses to which it is being put.

Furthermore, the increasing impact of individual Net Citizens (or 'Netizens') on capacity requirements, infrastructure investments and rollout, as well as on the evolution of internet services, is shifting cyber-power away from state and corporate players toward consumers at a rapid rate. This is best seen in the rise of social media, infotainment and e-Commerce, as outlined elsewhere in this book.

All this adds up to dependency without control and, as we know, dependency is the marker for our biggest risks.

Our globalised economic system is not the first of its kind, although it is certainly the largest in absolute terms. Nevertheless, the Romans, Chinese, Persians and several other civilisations had equivalent 'globalised' economic models, limited only by the boundaries of their respective expansions. A middle class citizen of the British Empire in the late 1800s no doubt found it unremarkable to sit down to a breakfast of Indian tea, sweetened by West Indian sugar alongside toast produced from American wheat, while reviewing South African gold prices in the daily newspapers.

What *is* truly unique about our modern version of globalisation is its total reliance on a shared and often insecure technology; the very dependency I refer to above. While we fully recognise the risks faced by all nations with respect to cyber security, we also note that globalisation in the twenty-first century is about far more than trade, payments and concepts of free markets and consumerism – it is about a vast, ubiquitous trans-national digital network,

off-shored customer data, and the globalised outsourcing of the related ICT
infrastructures and services.

THE SIX AGES OF WAR

I like to list six ages of war, as shown in Table 8.1. I break cyber-warfare out
from traditional signals intelligence on the basis that cyber-technologies and
infrastructure are revolutionary and they criss-cross civilian, governmental,
military and corporate boundaries in a pattern so complex and changeable that
it is probably impossible to map it completely. In a sense, we have returned
to an age of warfare that predates the geological survey, with military forces
operating in cyber space likely to find themselves as constrained and short on
accurate, timely and complete intelligence as those of Napoleon, Kutuzov, Sun
Tzu or Lee.

Table 8.1   The six ages of war

1st Age	2nd Age	3rd Age	4th Age	5th Age	6th Age
Land	Land	Land	Land	Land	Land
	Naval	Naval	Naval	Naval	Naval
		Signals	Signals	Signals	Signals
			Air	Air	Air
				Space	Space
					Cyber

Source: Johnson, 2011.

One key differentiator that marks the cyber warfare challenge out from all
others is the speed of change, both technological and infrastructural. With
billions of users and millions of domains, simply identifying new targets
and keeping track of existing ones is a truly daunting task. Faced with such a
challenge, a corporate body would immediately ask about the cost/benefit ratio
and national governments should perhaps consider equivalent questions.

EIGHT FACTORS AFFECTING CYBER WARFARE

There is a presumption among a large proportion of those thinking about this
topic that the conduct of cyber warfare between major powers is a given. At
the very least, it is assumed that a failure to develop a comprehensive defence

and retaliatory capability is a weakness that an enemy would naturally exploit, either in the form of a digital Pearl Harbour first strike, or as part of a wider conventional strategy.

One consequence of this mindset has been the rapid development of a cyber warfare arms race, similar in many ways to the nuclear arms race that took place during the mid-to-late twentieth century. Like the great mobilisations that occurred on the eve of the First World War, planning for cyber warfare is a potential trigger for that form of war in its own right, but this may be unavoidable. Listed below are eight key factors that, we postulate, combine to make a major cyber war between the world's great economic and military powers complex and potentially catastrophic, with hugely deleterious effects on communications providers and their corporate clients.

Globalisation – We All Sink or Swim Together

As stated repeatedly, twenty-first-century globalisation rests on a technological foundation. We are all aware of how devastating even a short-term loss of internet and communications services would be to corporate activity, national economic life and social cohesion. However, we seem to be less conscious of the impacts of such a technical failure on the globalised economy.

Consider a typical international bank structured along the lines of, say, an HSBC. The bank's own marketing images depict a global network of banking hubs and national branches, all interconnected and interdependent, handling financial transfers across borders, the accounts of globalised corporate clients and supported by outsourced ICT, call centres in India, the UK and the USA. No doubt the bank also utlises Cloud services in various forms.

This hypothetical bank does not exist in any one country – it exists globally. Launch a cyber attack on any major economy and you risk bringing down the whole bank, not only in the targeted state, but everywhere. Target the internet in, say India, and call centres supporting all of the bank's clients may go down at the same time.

Entanglement – Chaos Theory in action

Although the word entanglement is generally used to describe an inability to clearly separate legitimate military cyber targets from civilian ones (for which a system of 'markers' has been proposed), we see an even closer correlation with quantum entanglement.

Quantum entanglement refers to quantum particles that are so closely related and interdependent that it is impossible to describe the qualities and behaviour of one particle without taking the other into account. They may indeed be the same particle possessing different states at the same time, I believe. This is a powerful metaphor and it perfectly captures the unpredictable and extremely complex interdependencies present in the cyber technologies.

The internet today probably provides one of the best examples of Chaos Theory in action we could ask for. Attempting to bring down significant national internet assets without disrupting the whole system will be like trying to swat red butterflies in the dark without hurting the blue ones. In a wholesale cyber war we simply can't predict the cascade of effects emanating from a bilateral series of major cyber attacks, nor can we be certain about our ability to adequately control the attack tools used or to focus their energies with sufficient precision.

Detection and Response – Everything Cyber is Digitalised and Instantaneous Except Us

There are effectively two options for detection and response in any high technology risk environment:

- Respond automatically in real-time based on a predetermined set of rules or some form of artificial intelligence, thus surrendering our decision making responsibilities

- Provide information to a group of human decision makers who will take valuable minutes or even hours to complete their deliberations

The problem raised by cyber warfare is that the attack may be over in milliseconds, long before a human user even registers an alert on a screen, while automated responses are a very risky proposition, particularly if they include retaliatory cyber or kinetic strikes.

We have arrived at the place where technology, while not yet more intelligent than us, certainly outperforms us for speed of response and volumes of data processing and storage. The decision we will need to make is whether speed or reason are paramount, although if a major event does occur, this question may come to be purely academic. I certainly won't be able to call or email you to discuss and you won't be able to tell me that I got it right!

Attribution – Was it Really Them?

Clever internet criminals use spoofing all the time – to alter their email addresses, their domain names, IP addresses or equipment identities. The most advanced criminal operations will daisy chain or 'trombone' traffic across multiple devices and jurisdictions to conceal its origin. The notion that the cyber warfare unit of any modern state would attack another state and leave an easy to follow trail back to its own servers doesn't really merit consideration.

It almost goes without saying, therefore, that once detection has occurred, the really challenging part of the decision-making process will be attribution – determining who *really* attacked us. This, in turn, breaks down into sub-questions such as:

- Where did the attack come from geographically?

- If it was a distributed attack (possibly involving thousands or even millions of devices) can we accurately identify its root?

- Was the attack government sponsored or encouraged?

- Was the attack launched from the territory of the sponsor or from that of a third party?

- Should the responsible government have been able to detect it?

- Should they have been able to prevent it?

- How are they responding to it now?

It is difficult to envision this iterative decision-making process being carried out rapidly and it seems very probable that answers to some of these questions may never be had.

False Flag Attacks – Or Was it Those Guys Over There?

The previous paragraphs hint at the very real possibility of 'false flag attacks' – these being attacks by party A against B that are deliberately designed to implicate party C. There could be any number of motives for such action, ranging from the personal through the political or even the corporate.

Just a few of the relevant questions that will need to be addressed before a rational and informed decision can be made about how to retaliate are:

- Are there non-state actors who would want us to attribute the attack to a particular state?

- Are there other state actors who would want us to attribute the attack to a third state?

- Are there citizens within our own nation who would wish us to attribute the attack to another state, possibly for ideological reasons?

Game Theory – As it Applies to the Concept of 'Markers'

Simply put, the concept of 'markers' involves the multilateral electronic signposting of military and civilian internet nodes to ensure that potential adversaries adhere to, as yet, informal international rules of cyber warfare. However, leaving historical experience aside, a simple mind experiment rooted in Game Theory raises questions:

- Nation A and Nation B agree to define markers for valid civilian facilities within their respective internet infrastructures.

- Neither nation can be sure that the other is being completely honest and not marking a small selection of secret military facilities as civilian.

- So each nation dishonestly marks some of its most sensitive secret assets in this fashion, on the assumption that the other side must be doing the same if it has any sense at all.

- Once a single case of false marking is uncovered, the whole marker system is undermined, effectively meaning that it is probably doomed from the outset.

The degree of trust required between nations for the cyber warfare marker system to work is so high that it renders this self same marker system redundant; if we can develop that much trust with our competitors, why would we suppose that a major conflict is a realistic prospect? Let's just trade with them and be done.

Risk of Escalation – Who Else are We Hurting and What if They Join with the Enemy?

Once again, globalisation raises its anointed head. Once Country A decides that a cyber warfare attack on Country B is warranted, it must then consider the potential effects on countries C through Z. Some of these countries may be allies of Country A. Others may be neutral states that would side with Country B if their own cyber assets were attacked. Some will already be allied to Country B.

With offshore hosting and the ubiquity of Cloud services, military planners in Country A will be hard pressed to assure their leaders that a widespread cyber attack on B will not have harmful effects on third party states and their globalised corporate citizens. Country A must therefore be prepared for retaliation from multiple countries that were not the target of the original attack.

The 'Y' Generation – Social Media, Anti-social Media, Political Protest and Revolution

Generation Y, born between 1980 and 2000, are our 'Indigenous Netizens', who use communication technology with the same ease as their native languages to influence, persuade, socialise and create. Through their efforts, cultural boundaries have been eroded and geographical distance is no longer a hindrance. Social media platforms such as Twitter or Facebook have become virtual nation states, providing a platform where national ideals and movements can be solidified into an online ethos sparking action. Across the globe, Generation Y, a generation shaped by profound and unique global, environmental, social, technological, educational, political and parenting shifts, has influenced social and political revolutions using social media platforms as their headquarters, their massive and virally contagious social networks as the army and their tweets or posts as powerful ammunition to mobilise, coordinate and, most importantly, to radicalise their membership.

The psychological reach of a social media revolution can snowball, garnering the support of millions in an incredibly short time period. The Arab Spring serves as one of the Netizen's greatest demonstrations of their influence and their ability to trigger change. Other examples include challenges to corporate policy with regard to the treatment of people and the environment, and their influence on the global economy through social network messaging and response, a good example being the recent series of 'Twitter Storms' that have seen consumers attacking corporate performance.

As Indigenous Netizens, Generation Y has managed to harness its values and beliefs in order to demand political and cultural change. The citizens of these new virtual 'states' possess dual nationality; they are citizens of their respective geographic states, but at the same time many see themselves as members of a new form of cyber-nation that has no borders and which transcends cultural and political boundaries. How they might respond in the event of a cyber hot war that threatens to take away their online life is one of the key unknowns to be pondered by strategists and planners.

PREDICTING STATE SPONSORED CYBER ATTACKS

My view is that there are probably two key determinants in any assessment of the risk that any given state or non-state actor will launch a major unprovoked cyber warfare attack on a major power. These are:

- The cyber warfare capabilities of the potential attacker

- The attacker's dependency on the internet for its own economic survival

This is illustrated in the Figure 8.1 which suggests that states can be scored against these two criteria and placed in one of the four quadrants.

In a globalised world, very few states are likely to fall into the top left quadrant, a category that has advanced cyber warfare capabilities but also has very low levels of dependence on the internet for its economic survival. The groups that do fall into that category may be certain non-state actors and 'hactivists', suggesting that the main threats emanate from them and not from nation states.

In conclusion, a major cyber attack has always been a terrifying prospect but, in our globalised economic model, it is potentially lethal. Meanwhile, it is the non-state actor who poses the greatest threat.

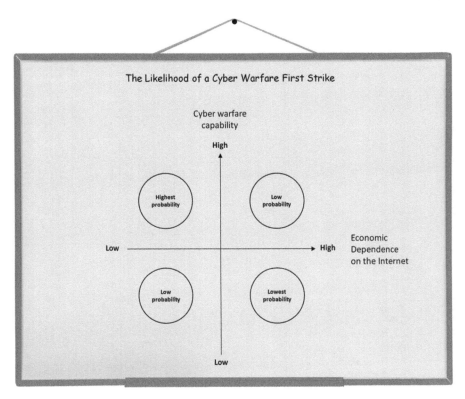

Figure 8.1   Assessing the likelihood of a cyber warfare first strike

9

Conclusion: Towards a Unifying Theory for Communications Risk

The complexity and diversity of manifest risks in communications services and infrastructure has created a spider's web of interconnections that link to almost every conceivable commercial and governmental activity, as well as having huge social implications. The internet itself is the best example, representing as it does a single point of failure for modern commerce, communications and national security, but many other risks also have impacts beyond the network.

Our years of work in this area have led us to develop a theory about risk in general that we will attempt to set out here. We theorise that in today's globalised, virtual, technical world (i.e. the social, cultural, economic and political spheres of life), the essence of risk can largely be described with three relatively simple sets of analysis:

- Dependency as a risk

- Risk management cycles

- A chaotic risk cascade

Dependency as a Risk

Contrary to conventional thinking on risk, where the relationship between frequency and impact is generally given as the primary mechanism for prioritising risk, we theorise that dependency is in fact the key parameter.

In assessing risks, we first need to identify the things upon which the entity being protected is entirely dependent. Two examples could be internet services and reputation, but you will no doubt be able to list others. Such dependency is in itself the key risk to any organisation. Risks of this nature, while clearly influenced in many cases by operational issues, are worthy of a different treatment from other operational risks such as subscriber fraud, billing inaccuracies and the like.

It is evident that the truly strategic risks to a business may well have operational roots and that the traditional separation of strategic vs. operational risk management issues may no longer be valid. In the modern world, dependency means that a lone teenage hacker crouched over a cheap PC in his bedroom might be your biggest strategic risk.

Taking this a step further, there appears to be a relationship between the numbers of users on our globalised ICT network or networks and the overall level of risk we face. This is an untested theory, but allow me to outline my thinking.

Firstly, it is apparent that as the cost of ownership falls (see Figure 9.1), the number of people acquiring mobile phones, tablets and laptops, as well as the

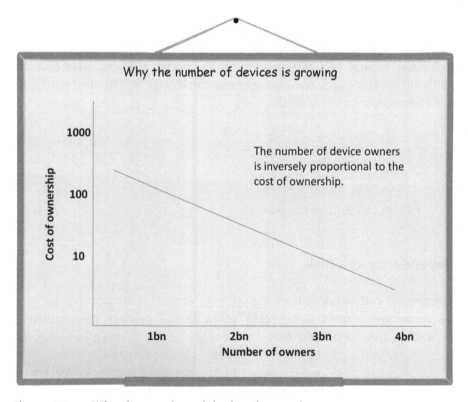

Figure 9.1   Why the number of devices is growing

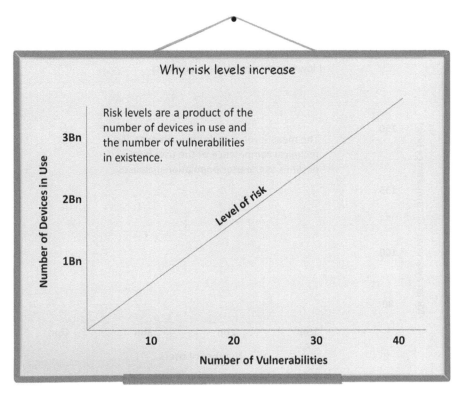

Figure 9.2   Why risk levels increase

broadband services that go with these systems, is rising rapidly. As cited earlier, some industry sources but the number of devices now connected to the Internet at 2.5 billion. Simply put, *the number of device owners is inversely proportional to the cost of ownership*. The significance of this fairly obvious statement will be explained by the statements that follow.

Secondly, there is a relationship between the number of devices (and users) on a network, the number of vulnerabilities that exist in relation to that network and the level of risk that exists on the network: more users combined with more vulnerabilities will result in a heightened level of risk (see Figure 9.2). So, we can say that *ICT Risk levels are a product of the number of devices in use and the number of vulnerabilities in existence*.

Finally, risks are balanced by controls and one of the key factors influencing the efficacy of controls is always going to be the security awareness and technical competence of users (see Figure 9.3). It doesn't matter how good your design is if you fail to design the idiot out of the system. In ICT terms, what we have

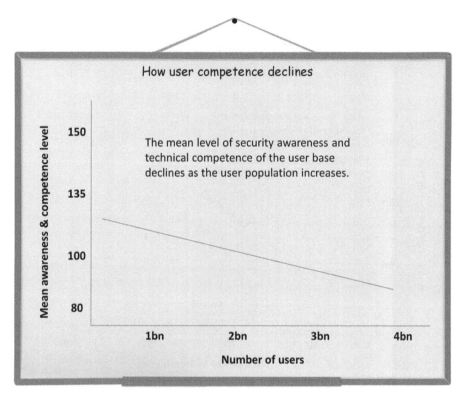

Figure 9.3   How mean user competence declines

witnessed over the last few decades is a simple progression from a situation in which most users (let's call them 'the first billion') were reasonably well educated and capable of being taught about security and best practice, to a 'second billion' who are less well educated and less able or willing to pay attention to security. We are now in the era of the 'third billion', many of whom are simply incapable of becoming security aware users of ICT technology. We can therefore say that *the mean level of security awareness and technical competence of the user base declines as the user population increases.* In spite of this, the industry has devolved more and more power into the hands of users, allowing them to install software, configure their devices and access remote systems like never before. This may prove to be the biggest of all contributors to ICT risk in the modern world.

Risk Management Cycles

Consultants and trainers have spent decades arguing about the perfect risk cycle and you will probably see many variations on the theme during your

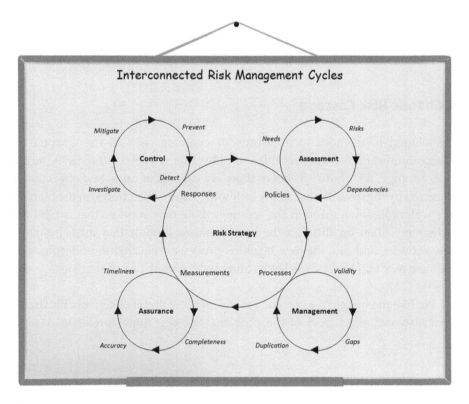

Figure 9.4   Interconnected risk management cycles

career. In a sense, it really doesn't matter greatly which version you choose as risk is a practice in a constant state of flux and it is possibly too complex and multifaceted to capture in a single diagram.

At the very least, risk management involves a series of interconnected cycles, each operating at different levels and speeds, but with each affecting how the others function. Looking at Figure 9.4, try to imagine that each cycle shown is in motion at a different speed as individuals or teams of people work through it, and as external factors impose friction to slow or accelerate the processes. Then imagine it in three dimensions, striped across multiple real world operations, locations, time zones and maturity levels. Hopefully, this will give you a glimpse of what communications risk management looks like in the wild.

Feel free to disagree with the labels I have used in the image and to replace them with as many substitutes as you wish. You can even add more cycles. The purpose of the image is to illustrate the complexity and interdependence of the collective risk management process, not to dictate the precise terms and sequences involved.

A Chaotic Risk Cascade

We alluded to the idea of a cascade of evolving risks in the Chapter on telecommunications fraud, yet this is an idea that relates to all risks in the era of technology. As Figure 9.5 shows, there is a cascade of cause and effect that is triggered by the invention of a new technology and which flows, in the manner of a waterfall, down through the creation of the new services that exploit the technology, then on through the new business models that arise from the new services, and into the new business processes required to underpin each business model. This cascade leads, ultimately, to new or variant risks.

We like the image of a cascade because we feel that it effectively illustrates the cause and effect facet of the problem, but you might prefer to draw it

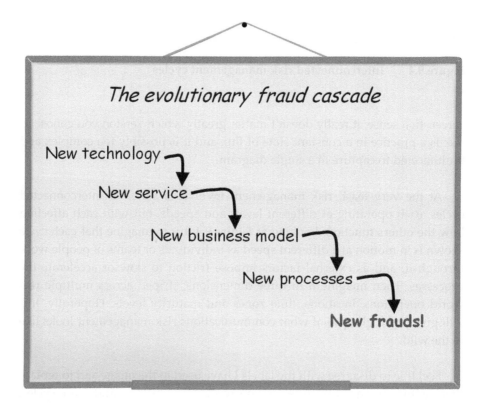

Figure 9.5   The risk cascade

differently. Whatever you do, bear in mind that the reality is fractal, in the sense that a single new technology (take 3G for example) can lead to many new services, each with slightly different business models and different processes. Also remember that those models are probably going to have to operate in different environments, with discrete possibilities for mitigating factors.

Chaos theory informs us that a slight change to the starting conditions will generally lead to wildly different conditions at the end of a given process. We can see why risk in modern communications services is chaotic and extremely difficult to forecast as a result.

This brings us back to the risk assessment challenge and how to assess the likelihood and impact of any given risk in the face of the chaotic risk cascade. The answer, we believe, is simple. Risks assessments need to include three primary types of analysis if they are to provide useful outputs in the modern world:

- *Needs analysis*: before evaluating risks, you must first evaluate the *need* the organisation has for the services or products under review. Without a proper sense of the needs or business benefits offered by a product or service, you will be unable to comment sensibly on the balance of risk and reward. If you focus solely on the risk side of the equation, leaving analysis of potential rewards to others, you jeopardise your position within the organisation and may be viewed as a harbinger of doom.

- *Dependencies analysis*: consider the dependencies the organisation has on relevant technologies or attributes and how these might be exposed to risk. These are your primary areas of risk.

- *Risk analysis*: consider the other risks that might manifest themselves and use historical data, data analytics, scenario analysis and brainstorming to assess their potential frequency and impact and the controls required to address each. Repeat these assessments regularly.

Your final risk assessment report will thus balance needs against risks and highlight the key dependencies that could bring things to a complete halt, while also providing a breakdown of the operational risks and controls required to maintain efficiency and profitability. These assessments need to be repeated

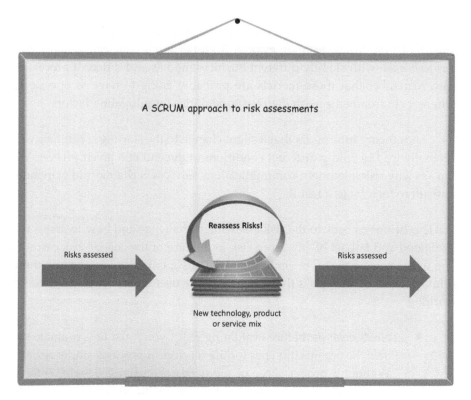

Figure 9.6   SCRUM approach to risk assessments

regularly as new technologies and services are introduced in a variation of the SCRUM project model (Figure 9.6).

In the SCRUM approach to risk assessments, there is a continuous process of risk assessment and re-assessment, reflecting the dynamic and fluid nature of our environment. Risks are scored, as explained earlier, and the highest scoring risks are re-assessed most frequently. Lower scoring risks are assessed at correspondingly lower frequencies, but every area at risk is re-assessed at least once a year and any new risks identified are added. This ensures that the risk register is a living document and that improvements to controls or increases in the levels of risk in any given area are observed and reflected in the register in a timely manner.

Throughout the book you will have noted our continuing reference to cycles: fraud and RA control cycles, risk management cycles, the recurring cascade of emerging risks as new technologies arrive on the scene. Communications risk management is an ever changing, always stimulating area of work, yet almost every new risk that arrives seems to have its roots in an older, well understood form of fraud, leakage or attack. This is good news. By learning the lessons of the past, we can anticipate many of the risks and challenges we will face in the future, and even those that are entirely new and unprecedented will be more easily understood. No matter how complex our ICT technologies become, it seems certain that most risks will either stem from human desires and motives, or from systems and process issues, and these can be quickly understood by anyone with a good grasp of the history. To steal a line from my favourite musician:

> *Don't forget your history; know your destiny: In the abundance of water, the fool is thirsty.*

> *Bob Marley, from the song* Rat Race,
> *from the* Album Rastaman Vibration

Index

Please note: references to Figures, Tables, Examples and Case Studies are shown in bold.

For Product Safety Concerns and Information please contact our
EU representative GPSR@taylorandfrancis.com Taylor & Francis
Verlag GmbH, Kaufingerstraße 24, 80331 München, Germany